THE IMPACT
OF HOME INTERNET ACCESS
ON TEST SCORES

THE IMPACT
OF HOME INTERNET ACCESS
ON TEST SCORES

Steve Macho

CAMBRIA PRESS

YOUNGSTOWN, NEW YORK

Library of Congress Cataloging-in-Publication Data
Macho, Steve.
    The impact of home Internet access on test scores / Steve Macho.
        p. cm.
    Includes bibliographical references and index.
    ISBN 978-1-934043-28-8 (alk. paper)
    1. Educational tests and measurements—Social aspects—United States—Case studies.
    2. Digital divide—United States—Case studies. I. Title.

    LB3051.M273 2007
    371.26'2—dc22

    2007005617

To the Lorraines: Jackson & Macho

TABLE OF CONTENTS

LIST OF FIGURES

LIST OF TABLES

LIST OF APPENDICES

FOREWORD

This research addresses an issue that concerns all of us, relating directly to the vitality of public education and to the future of our democratic society. Presented in this study is further evidence of the continuing negative impacts on the academic achievement of those students lacking home access to the Internet and the educational resources recognized as necessary for an adequate education. Those students in secondary education without Internet access at home are disadvantaged—a scenario that strikes at the foundations of public education.

Explicit in the rationale for public education in the United States is the preparation of a knowledgeable society who will ensure the preservation of their social structure. This intent was clear in the words of one of this country's notable founders, Thomas Jefferson, who stated "I know no safe depository of the ultimate powers of the society but the people themselves; and if we think them not enlightened enough to exercise their control with a wholesome discretion, the remedy is not to take it from them, but to inform them their discretion by education" (Thomas Jefferson to William C. Jarvis, 1820).

There is a strong correlation between a literate citizenry and a successful democracy. Public education, recognizing that education is the bedrock of any successful democracy, strives to develop a literate citizenry—one that can think for itself, reason, critique, and analyze. This pathway to literacy requires an educational system that can provide the necessary resources to educate every citizen within this system—a task increasingly difficult in the 20th century. Gone are the days when those necessary resources could be housed within the confines of select physical structures such as local schools and libraries. In the current digital era these necessary resources are increasingly housed in global electronic networks available anywhere, anytime to any connected computer. This raises the issue of access, commonly referred to as the digital divide, which has direct implications for our ability to maintain equal educational opportunities for all—the key to preparing a knowledgeable citizenry.

Evidence for a direct causal relationship between student achievement and access to the body of information available through electronic means is difficult to establish due to the many confounding social variables. Social science does not lend itself well to true experimental design and discrete causal relationships. However, in this carefully designed quasi-experimental research, Dr. Macho uses an alternative approach to investigating digital divide issues relative to a select few classic factors of academic achievement. His thorough analysis of confounding variables contained within a large extant database provides a significant contribution to our further understanding of the interplay between Internet access at home and a host of variables known to contribute to academic achievement.

The significance of this research should not be underestimated. The need to ensure equal access by secondary level students to the growing body of digital educational resources is more critical than ever, and will remain so in the foreseeable future. This research is a significant addition to the body of knowledge regarding the effects of Internet access on the learning process, and provides policy makers, school administrators and classroom teachers with evidence of the importance of such access. For those concerned with the inequities of resources attributed to a digital divide that threatens the preparation of a literate citizenry, the basis of our democratic society, this research is a must read.

Professor John G. Wells
Virginia Polytechnic Institute and State University

PREFACE

The research question of this study—what are the differences among the standardized test scores of students due to factors of *Internet access at home, household income*, and *highest level of education attained by mother, father, or guardian*—is a somewhat different question than is typically posed in consideration of the effects of the Internet on learning. Vendors are typically asserting their Internet-based product as having a positive effect unachievable with alternate approaches, or advocates and practitioners of pedagogies are measuring a proposed effect with the added ingredient of "Internet."

A concern with issue of inquiry into the effect of technology on learning is that random assignment is all but practically impossible when conducting research on "real kids." Quasi-experimental methods are loaded with issues regarding lack of control (or even identification) of external factors.

As opposed to proving an expected effect due to Internet access, the following study surveys a selection of classic factors of academic performance contrasted to those with and without Internet in the home.

In simple analysis, the data revealed that having Internet access at home is significant. In fact, in simple analysis, every factor in the study was found to be significant as well. When confounding factors were considered, however, Internet access became insignificant. Thorough analysis demonstrated that differences in achievement are far more closely related to the education of the parent or guardian.

The danger of a result that is *significant* in the absence of other factors may lead to the endorsement of a spurious association. In this research, the spurious association would be: the presence of Internet in the home is associated with higher academic standing. This statement rings true only when one considers reality with reckless abandon.

Since the completion of this study in 2005, other research-based publications support the findings, specifically, that the quality of the research is enhanced by consideration of confounding factors.

Jackson, von Eye, Biocca, Barbatsis, and Zhao (2006) published in a recent issue of *Developmental Psychology* an article titled "Does Home Internet Use Influence the Academic Performance of Low-Income Children?" The authors state that, in their review of the literature, "Available evidence suggests that having a home computer is linked to somewhat better academic performance, although most studies fail to control for factors that covary with having a home computer (e.g., parental income and education)" (¶ 11). Their research did consider race and patterns of Internet use as a confounding factor in the analysis, and their results indicate that "Children who used the Internet more during the last four months of the project had higher GPAs and standardized test scores in reading than did children who used it less" (Discussion section, ¶ 1). Research such as this, which considers confounding factors, presents more exact insight into the complexity of understanding the effects of Internet access on learning.

The issues expressed regarding the notion of the digital divide—that an inequity of resources may perpetuate and exacerbate social divisions—is a key aspect to this research. *The Digital Divide and Academic Achievement*, published by Huang and Russell (2006), states:

> The findings show that the digital divide still exists, cutting through various socioeconomic factors, and that the relationship between technology accessibility and academic achievement may also exist, although it is very much complicated by other compounding factors, such as the subjects

of learning, the uses of technology, and socioeconomic conditions. (¶ 2)

It is my hope that future research will continue to diversify its consideration of confounding factors and hence produce a more comprehensive understanding of the actual effect that Internet access in the home has on student achievement.

ACKNOWLEDGMENTS

A special thanks to my father, Vernon Macho, for setting an example of life long learning—while he achieved the "normal" eighth-grade education of rural-Minnesota in the early 1940s—in the 1970s he brought me along to his night classes when he became an engineer. Also, for being raised the fourth generation on a family farm, which provides lessons far beyond the scope of any formal education experiences.

The influences of many hands are in this book; this is an abridged collection of their names. In West Virginia: Dr. Ed Pytlik, Dr. John Wells, Dr. Dick Walls, Dr. Sebastian Diaz, Dr. Stacy Gartin, Dr. Ernest Goeres, Dr. Dave McCrory, Dr. Paul DeVore, and Dr. George Maughn. In the New Mexico and other various places: Jose C'de Baca "*saint Joe*" (New Mexico Highlands University-GEARUP), Abad Sandoval (Los Alamos National Laboratory–STB / UO), Dr. Chris Nelson (New Mexico Highlands University–School of Education), Dr. Pat and Rosena Romero (retired NMHU Technology Education Chair), Dr. David West, Dr. Jim Abreu (both at NMHU), Dr. Bill Robertson (University of Texas at El Paso–School of Education), Joe Vigil (Los Alamos National Laboratory–SEO), and Dr. Paul Siciliano (of the entire world). From the earlier years: Dr. Andy Horton (of his beloved Appalachians)—Andy set this all in motion by removing barriers I had made, Dr. "Bud" Nestle and Dr. Anthony Akubue

(St Cloud State University), and Dr. Stan Edin (Staples Technical Institute) who reminded me that I was a sum of my choices.

A special thanks to my wife, Cate—essentially; this book would not exist without her influences, the dream would have been abandoned.

Finally, I want to thank Cambria Press.

THE IMPACT
OF HOME INTERNET ACCESS
ON TEST SCORES

CHAPTER ONE

INTRODUCTION

Technologies in the home, such as computers and Internet access, have become common in the past decade. In 2002, over half of all Americans were using the Internet (U.S. Department of Commerce, 2002). Nearly every student in the United States has used the Internet for schoolwork (Lenhart, Simon, & Graziano, 2001; Levin & Arafeh, 2002; U.S. Department of Commerce, 2002; U.S. Department of Education, 2005a).

> Many parents purchase computers expressly for their children's educational use. Access to the Internet has been one of the driving forces for this growth, which is expected to continue in the coming years, especially as options for faster connections to the Internet become more common, through cable services and high speed telephone access. Greater access to home computers is being encouraged by increasingly less expensive computers (below $1000) that invite moderate income families, often first-time users, to acquire technology. (Kafai, Fishman, Bruckman, & Rockman, 2002, p. 53)

How are students using this resource for educational purposes? "Approximately 9 out of 10 high school students who have access to a home computer use that computer to complete school assignments" (Fairlie, 2003, p. 3). The National Center for Educational Statistics published, *Computer and Internet Use by Children and Adolescents in 2001 Statistical Analysis Report* (2003) and reports of 5–17-year-old students: 68% indicate they have accessed the Internet from the school, 78% indicate they have accessed the Internet from home, and 46% use the Internet to complete school assignments (pp. vi, 22).

A survey of 754 students, who were 12–17 year olds, conducted by the Pew Internet & American Life Project, reports that 94% of those who have Internet access state they use it for school research and 78% state they believe the Internet helps them with schoolwork. Most students (71%) report that they have used the Internet as a "major source for their most recent major school project or report (Lenhart et al., 2001, p. 2)." About half (41%) use email for school purposes, and about one-third (34%) have downloaded a study guide. Roughly three in five (58%) have used web sites made for one of their classes. About one in five (17%) have created web pages for school projects, and (18%) know of someone who has "used the Internet to cheat on a paper or test (Lenhart et al., 2001, p. 2)." These findings support the notion that Internet use has an impact on student learning, and hence, measured performance.

Schoolwork is not the only use of the Internet resource within the home. The U.S. Department of Commerce (2002) and the U.S. Department of Education (Rathbun, West, & Hausken, 2003) rank educational uses of home Internet access as the second most popular use, behind gaming. Is the secondary use of the Internet, homework, of consequence to student performance? A September 2004 publication, *Technology and Equity in Schooling: Deconstructing the Digital Divide* (Warschauer & Knobel, 2004), questions the contribution of technology access in the home. Specifically, Warschauer and Knobel state, "Although home access to computers has long been regarded as important for supporting students' academic achievement, research suggests that home ownership of computers alone does not level out inequalities in terms of technology's contributions to student learning" (p. 563).

The common perception questioned by Warschauer and Knobel is a vision of students refining their homework at home with the new marvel.

"Public school children who had access to home computers used them on an average of three to four days a week. Over 85% of young children with home computers used them for educational purposes" (Rathbun et al., 2003, p. 12). "Some may believe that inexpensive computing devices will provide ubiquitous access for all students, at home and in school" (Kafai et al., 2002, p. 65). With more computers placed in homes, should we expect students to perform better in school? It appears that it is not quite that simple.

> we recognized (as previous researchers did) that computers alone are not the central factor in making educational computing at home and its connection to school work. Any effort needs to consider not only activities and resources in schools but also families and their available resources both at home and in their communities (Kafai et al., 2002, p. 65).

Some research has indicated that there is an association between the availability of a computer and Internet access in the home and student performance. As stated in *The Information Society* article by Attewell and Battle of City University of New York, Home Computers and School Performance (1999), "We find that having a home computer is associated with higher test scores in mathematics and reading" (p. 1). Sweeping statements such as *home computers are being associated with higher test scores* may be true, but the depth of that truth may be an issue. The particular issue with this reasoning is the danger of putting forth conclusions based upon a spurious association.

Milo Schield, Professor at Augsburg College in Minneapolis, has published numerous articles on the topic of critically considering the use of statistics and the appropriate inferences that can be made from their application. Schield provides the following definition of a spurious association:

> To understand a spurious association, one must understand Simpson's Paradox. A spurious association is both *true* and *false*—but in different ways. It is true given what one has (or has not) taken into account (controlled for). It is 'false' or at least accidental because it does not persist

after one takes into account (controls for) a more important confounding factor (Schield, 1999, p. 5).

When trying to correctly qualify—or quantify—if there is an effect of home Internet access on student academic standing, other factors must be taken into consideration. Schield advises the consideration of three explanations of the factors being considered to explain a phenomenon:

> one must review three different kinds of explanations for any association obtained from an observational study. In interpreting an observational association between A and B, the three causal explanations are (1) A causes B, (2) B causes A, and (3) C (some confounding factor) causes both A and B. Once all three explanations are expressed, one can work at eliminating one and supporting another (Schield, 1999, p. 5).

To determine if there is an association of Internet access at home and academic standing, other factors need to be included in the research design. The research design should determine differences and potential interactions among factors such as Internet access at home, family affluence, and academic achievement. Applying these three tests to the design of the study can lead to the following statements:

1. The presence of Internet access in the home causes a higher test score;
2. Higher test scores cause the presence of the Internet at home; or
3. Other factors such as family affluence (family income, parents level of education), explain both differences in academic standing and the presence of Internet access at home.

Each of these three explanations, patterned after Schields' explanations, has potential and supporting arguments with varied degrees of merit or legitimacy. To declare that the presence of Internet access at home is the sole cause of academic standing is to deny all other potential mitigating factors. The second explanation could be that the students with greater academic standing place a higher value on the use of computers and Internet access, and have therefore manipulated their environment to include that resource in their home. The third explanation seems like the most likely and is a model for the research question proposed within this study. With the third explanation in mind, a statistical method can be chosen which will examine the differences and interactions among the contribution of the factors; that is, the independent variables' effect on the dependent variable.

There are bodies of evidence to support the notion of family affluence being associated with student performance and Internet access. The National Center for Educational Statistics Scholastic Assessment, *Test score averages, by selected student characteristics: 1995–1996, 1997–1998, and 1999–2000* (Table 135, 2004) clearly illustrates the trend that student scores tend to increase relative to household income. The association of parent education and student academic performance are supported by nearly 30 years worth of data from the National Center for Educational Statistics, *Average student scale score in reading, by age and selected student and school characteristics: Selected years, 1971 to 1999* (Table 110, 2004). The notion that household income and Internet access are related are supported by data from the U.S. Department of Commerce, *Internet use among 10 to 17 year olds by income and location, 2001* (2002). These factors of family affluence impact upon academic standing are already established.

An optimal research design would control for *all* other potential factors; such as an experimental design. In an ideal experimental design, all variables would be quantified; that is, factors ranging from the attitude and physical condition of the students, situational circumstances in a classroom, availability of computer and Internet resources in the home, assurance that those resources are in proper working condition, that all parents would treat all students equally, and that each teacher would treat each student equally. Everything a student encounters would be equitable with all other students with the only exception being Internet access within the home. It would be exceedingly difficult to use an experimental design where households would be controlled and randomly assigned to have or not have computer and Internet access. Therefore, an experimental design would be difficult to employ to determine the effect of home and Internet access on student standing.

Data utilizing established factors of family affluence and standardized test results were available from the San Miguel GEARUP Partnership. The San Miguel GEARUP Partnership is conducted in Las Vegas, New Mexico, at New Mexico Highlands University. Parents of participants complete an application form annually. The Appendix *NMHU / San Miguel GEAR-UP Student Application, 2003–2004 School Year*, contains a reproduction of the survey form. The data collected from this instrument were used to conduct the GEARUP program and complete an annual performance review. There was a high rate of return on the applications because completed applications were required before any students could obtain their earned reward. The participant's application form contained questions that were within the scope of the objectives of GEARUP, for example, Do you plan to go on to college? What college? What major? Data gathered by the San Miguel GEARUP partnership includes information on Internet access at home and family affluence. The San Miguel GEARUP partnership has collected the results of standardized tests on participants.

Using data from the San Miguel GEARUP partnership is in the interest of the partnership because findings of this study could be used to seek support to provide Internet access to San Miguel GEARUP partnership participants in hopes of improving their academic standing. Findings of this research could be generalized to other underrepresented populations similar to those of the San Miguel GEARUP partnership.

A quasi-experimental research design can be selected to determine if there is a difference in the academic standing for those who have Internet access at home compared to those who do not have Internet access at home. Although those with Internet access at home may have a different academic standing, is that an indication of family affluence or a benefit of that technology, or some combination of both? Therefore, the effect of family affluence will be examined to determine if a potential difference in academic standing is an independent factor, or if it follows family affluence. Affluence for the purposes of this study will be defined as the income level of the household the student resides within, and the highest attained education levels of the mother, father, or guardian.

PURPOSE OF THE STUDY

Prior research (Attewell & Battle, 1999; Becker, 2000; Warschauer & Knobel, 2004) indicates that there are relationships between technology access at home and a difference in standardized test scores. There are also findings that associate family affluence with differences in standardized test scores (Levin & Arafeh, 2002; National Center for Educational Statistics Scholastic Assessment, 2003 & 2004). The purpose of this study is to investigate potential differences in student academic standing between those with Internet access at home and those without Internet access at home, and to take into consideration the potential confounding factors of family affluence. Family affluence, specifically, will be defined as household income, and the highest education level of an immediate relative (mother, father, or guardian). These factors of family affluence are selected because a large body of research from the National Center for Educational Statistics Scholastic Assessment indicates an association of difference in standardized test scores and these factors.

Findings of this research could help us understand the value of Internet access at home. Findings could also support policies to promote home Internet access in the interest of improving student performance.

PROCEDURES OF THE STUDY

1. Identify, refine, and develop the problem for the focus of the research;
2. Review the literature of computer and Internet use at home, family affluence as it relates to students academic standing, research methods, and statistical methods;
3. Identify the methods to determine if any significant differences exist among the factors;
4. Query the San Miguel GEARUP Partnership database for the data to perform the tests;
5. Conduct analysis of measured results and;
6. Draw conclusions from analysis;
7. Present findings, conclusions, and recommendations.

ASSUMPTIONS

The following assumptions are made in this study:

1. Assumes the self-reported data on the San Miguel GEARUP Partnership applications are accurate;

2. The data input process was accurate and the data in the database are accurate;
3. Assumes the CTB / McGraw-Hill–TerraNova provided an accurate and valid test score;
4. Other factors not considered apply equally to all of the students in the study.

DEFINITION OF TERMS

Internet—Global networks connecting millions of computers. More than 100 countries are linked into exchanges of data, news and opinions (Webopedia, 2004, ¶ 1).

Globally Unique Identifier (GUID)—A unique 128-bit number that is produced by the Windows OS or by some Windows applications to identify a particular component, application, file, database entry, and / or user (Webopedia, 2004, ¶ 1).

Normal Curve Equivalent (NCE) Score—The NCE was developed to allow mathematical manipulation of National Percentile (NP) scores—especially for program evaluation and research requiring the comparison of scores across groups or across time. The NCE scores can be thought of as NP scores rescaled on an equal interval scale (which allows them to be used in mathematical calculations such as deriving a mean score) (Indiana Department of Education, 2005; Normal Curve Equivalent (NCE) Score section, ¶ 1).

CTB / McGraw-Hill–TerraNova—The TerraNova is the standardized test adopted by the State of New Mexico for use in all schools. This is a norm-referenced test (McGraw-Hill, 2004, ¶ 2).

San Miguel GEARUP Partnership—Located in rural Northeastern New Mexico the NMHU / San Miguel GEARUP Project is a U.S. Department of Education five-year grant designed to increase the number of low-income students who will be prepared to enter and succeed in college. GEARUP serves an entire cohort of students beginning in the sixth grade and following them as a cohort through the completion of high school (U.S. Department of Education, 2004).

San Miguel GEARUP Partnership database—The San Miguel GEARUP Partnership has developed a database containing the program information necessary to conduct the initiatives set forth by the funding agency. The Database has evolved from a series of spreadsheets to a Microsoft Access relational database and the current state as a fully normalized MS-SQL 2000 database. The primary sources of data in the database are demographics collected from participant parents and academic and behavioral data entered by teachers. Imported data sources include results of standardized tests, state content standards and benchmarks, and educational objectives.

CHAPTER TWO

BACKGROUND

STUDENTS AND THE INTERNET

"One of the most common activities that youth perform online is schoolwork," specifically, 94% of 12 to 17 year olds who use the Internet, report that they used it for schoolwork (Levin & Arafeh, 2002, p. 1). This widespread use of the Internet is likely to impact student learning. The resource of the Internet is fundamentally different from other educational resources because it does not require physical access to the school (e.g., independent of space and time). Internet savvy students can perform their schoolwork independent of time restrictions because they can access school resources for their homework independent of the hours of operation for the school. Internet savvy students can access resources independent of physical space. They can access school resources for their homework independent of the physical location of the school. Breaking the barriers of space and time is a part of the value the Internet delivers to all of its users. This potentially meaningful access to the Internet is however dependent upon the access existing for the students when they are not in school but presumably at home.

Almost every public school student in the United States has access to the Internet (U.S. Department of Commerce, 2004). However, Internet access at home is not as universal. It is assumed those who have Internet access at home are at an advantage versus those who do not have Internet access; this has been coined as the *Digital Divide*. The concept of a Digital Divide was a guiding principle for policy development and enactment in the late 1990s.

Following the Digital Divide, educational policices focused on the No Child Left Behind Act, which holds that all students should perform at a common standard, and the required resources to achieve that goal should be provided. With regards to Internet access for students, providing Internet access within schools is typically considered the enactment of this policy. An exception is the Evaluation of Student & Parent Access through Recycled Computers (eSPARC) program funded by the U.S. Department of Education in 2004 and conducted by the Pennsylvania State Department of Education. This three-year program is designed to study the "impact of computer technology and its benefits to students and families" (Pennsylvania State Department of Education, 2004, ¶ 2). This research identifies qualified participants, provides them training, gathers baseline data, and provides refurbished computers to high-need families.

In the late 1990s, most schools had some sort of limited Internet access, and consequentially, so did most students. Financial budgets dictated whether schools would have Internet access; as a result, the schools that did have Internet access at this introductory stage were the ones in more affluent communities. This also applied to training for teachers on using the Internet and teaching students about it.

From 2000 to 2005, there has been an impressive adoption of networks within schools. Net-days, E-rate, and other such programs have assisted in the creation of a network infrastructure that span nearly every American school. In addition to the existence of the physical infrastructure, a knowledge base to maintain these systems is becoming more common within schools. There have been several iterations of Internet-based software which has transformed the nature of interacting with information. Distributed network applications had become commonplace from 2000 to 2004. All of these factors have contributed to the creation of an environment that is compelling students to interact. "A July 2002 survey by the Pew Internet & American Life Project shows that three in five children under the age of 18—and more than 78% of children between the ages of 12 and 17—go online" (Levin & Arafeh, 2002, p. ii).

> In the last decade, the federal, state, and local governments have invested over $40 billion to put computers in schools and connect classrooms to the Internet. Results are positive related to hardware and connectivity. The percentage of schools connected to the Internet rose from 35% in 1994 to 99% in 2001. The student to Internet connected computer ratio has improved dramatically in an even shorter time frame, going from 12 students per computer in 1998 to five to one in 2001. Many students who do not have computer and Internet access at home at least have some access at school. (Dickard, 2003, p. 7)

MAGNITUDE OF STUDENT USE OF THE INTERNET

As stated in the U.S. Department of Education (2005) national technology plan *Toward a New Golden Age in American Education: How the Internet, the Law and Today's Students are Revolutionizing Expectations*, "94 percent of online teens use the Internet for school-related research" (p. 17). However, the scope of the growth of the Internet seems to break traditionally established lines.

> Internet use is increasing for people regardless of income, education, age, races, ethnicity, or gender. Between December 1998 and September 2001, Internet use by individuals in the lowest income households (those earning less than $15,000 per year) increased at a 25 percent annual growth rate. Internet use among individuals in the highest-income households (those earning $75,000 per year or more) increased from a higher base but at a much slower 11 percent annual growth rate. (U.S. Department of Commerce, 2002, p. 1)

The growth of Internet usage is likely to continue until nearly every American is online. According to the U.S. Department of Commerce (2002) "children and teenagers use computers and the Internet more than any other age group" (p. 1). They state that "Ninety percent of children between the ages of 5 and 17 (or 48 million) now use computers" (p. 1), "Seventy-five percent of 14–17 year olds and 65 percent of 10–13 year olds use the Internet" (p. 1), and "Family households with children under the age of 18 are more likely to access the Internet" (p. 1).

A survey of 754 students who were 12–17 year olds, performed by Lenhart et al. in 2001 for The Pew Internet & American Life Project, reports that 94% of the students who have Internet access say they have used it for school research and 78% say they believe the Internet helps them with schoolwork. Most students (71%) report that they have used the Internet as a "major source for their most recent major school project or report" (p. 2). About half (41%) use email for school purposes, and about one-third (34%) have downloaded a study guide. Roughly, three in five (58%) have used web sites made for one of their classes. About one in five (17%) have created web pages for school projects, and about one in five (18%) know of someone who has "used the Internet to cheat on a paper or test" (p. 2).

Further research by Rathbun et al., for the National Center for Education Statistics, Institute of Education Sciences, U.S. Department of Education indicates that "Public school children who had access to home computers used them on an average of three to four days a week. Over 85% of young children with home computers used them for educational purposes" (2003, p. 12).

ASSUMPTION THAT TECHNOLOGY IN THE HOME HAS AN EFFECT ON ACADEMIC STANDING

While access to the technology is available, and studies indicate that students are making use of both computers and Internet for schoolwork, what *exactly* does that mean? The factors and results of research on this issue, what is *known about student use of the Internet for schoolwork*, are presented in this section of the Literature review. Research on technology used by students did not include the effect that home Internet access may have on academic standing. In fact "large-scale research on school-related uses of the Internet—as distinguished from research on the use of computers and other technologies—has focused on access" (Levin & Arafeh, 2002, p. 2) and then not the assumed effect on academic performance.

Digital Divide and Policy Issues

The essence of the Digital Divide is based upon an assumption that the differential access to communications technology exacerbates social differences between *haves* and *have-nots* (Becker, 2000). In the late 1990s, this perceived difference became the impetus for a socially sensitive communications policy. In hope of *bridging* the access gap, many programs were created and supported by both government agencies and private entities. Most of the efforts, such as E-Rate, and Net-Day, were focused on providing assistance with physical facilities and equipment or the expenses associated with initiation of networks services (Becker, 2000; U.S. Department of Education, 2005b). Stated in *A Retrospective on Twenty Years of Education Technology Policy*, by 1997, "As the Internet began to emerge, recommendations regarding access addressed the need for Internet connections in addition to the hardware and software" (McMillan-Culp, Honey, & Mandinach, 2003, p. 11). These efforts were for the most part successful, as of now nearly every student in the United States has access to the Internet at school.

By 2005, access to the Internet was assumed to be standard for all students. The U.S. Department of Education cites priorities in the national technology plan, *Toward a New Golden Age in American Education: How the Internet, the Law and Today's Students are Revolutionizing Expectations*, released on January 7, 2005. The only recommended technical initiatives stated as priorities in the national technology plan were to encourage broadband access, promote technical teacher training, and integrate data systems.

The expectation of universal access is expressed in the actions of the U.S. Department of Education. The registration document for the June 2003 event, *Education Technology: Preparing Students and Parents for the Digital Age*, states "Technology has tremendous potential to inspire students, improve academic performance, and close the achievement gap for children who historically have been left behind" (U.S. Department of Education, 2003, ¶ 1). The web-based workshop, which was only available to those who *have* Internet access, clearly draws the connection between the potential of a parent to participate in their child's education and the availability of technology.

This registration document for the June 2003 event also illustrates another important aspect that may be potentially exacerbated, parent access to the students' education process. The parents' role in the notion of the digital divide is important in two ways: providing access for themselves (the parent) to participate in the education process, and providing the technology in the home for their child to use as a learning tool. Most parents believe in providing Internet access, as indicated by the findings of The Pew Internet & American Life Project.

> Parents agree with their online children that Internet helps with learning. Fully 93% believe that the Internet helps children learn new things. Eighty-seven percent of these parents say the Internet helps children with their schoolwork. And 95% of these parents say it is important for children to learn about the Internet in order to be a success later in life; 55% say it is essential. (Lenhart et al., 2001, p. 4)

The use of the Internet not only supports the students' activities; it also helps the parents as directors of their children's learning. Those without access to these technology resources will be at a disadvantage compared to those who have Internet access at home.

> Technology has also become a powerful tool to help parents stay involved in their child's education. School Web sites, message boards and the like now provide mothers and fathers with access to everything from assignments and lunch menus to specific information on their children's academic performance and offer an almost infinite number of learning resources. (U.S. Department of Education, 2003, ¶ 2)

As a result, parents who have home Internet access can be active participants in their students' academic life beyond attending parent teacher conferences. They can communicate with their child's teachers and may take part in the curriculum and do a better job of helping their children with homework, because they can go on line and see the homework. Likewise, there is an improvement in the flow of information from the school to home, from the teachers, and other practitioners to the parents concerning their children's needs. Internet access can help generate a dialogue so that parents and teachers need not wait for the semi-annual parent teacher meeting in order to do so.

Student Behavior Using the Internet

The ways students use the Internet within the home can be observed and has been the topic of several studies. The behaviors students exhibit when making use of the Internet at home are an important aspect of study because they are in part the behaviors that are suspected to lead to a different academic standing. While there are studies that indicate students use the Internet to perform *schoolwork* (Becker, 2000; Lenhart et al., 2001; Levin & Arafeh, 2002; U.S. Department of Commerce, 2002; U.S. Department of Education, 2002, 2003) the qualities of the use are described differently. The literature also typically agreed with the notion that teachers had reservations about assigning homework that would require home Internet use. Teachers underestimate how many students have access at home, and as a consequence lower their expectations of all students in an attempt to be fair to those without Internet access at home (Lenhart et al., 2001; Levin & Arafeh, 2002).

The Pew Internet & American Life Project has published the results of their research efforts regarding what students are doing with Internet access. Two studies of interest are *The Internet & Education* Lenhart et al. (2001), and *The Digital Disconnect: The Widening Gap between Internet-Savvy Students and their Schools* by Levin & Arafeh (2002). The research methods for both of these publications involved survey research. *The Internet & Education* (2001) was based upon a survey of 754 teenagers (ages 12–17) who used the Internet including a parent or guardian and was "conducted by Princeton Survey Research Associates between November 2, 2000 and December 15, 2000" (p. 9) with a margin of error of plus or minus 4%.

Notable among the 2002 study is the finding that "Internet-savvy students rely on the Internet to help them do their schoolwork" (Levin & Arafeh, 2002, p. 26). This notion is central to the assumption that students with

Internet access at home have the potential to perform better than those without Internet access. Levin and Arafeh go on to state:

> Students told us they complete their schoolwork more quickly; they are less likely to get stymied by material they don't understand; their papers and projects are more likely to draw upon up-to-date sources and state-of-the-art knowledge; and, they are better at juggling their school assignments and extracurricular activities when they use the Internet. In essence, they told us that the Internet helps them navigate their way through school and spend more time learning in depth about what is most important to them personally. (Levin & Arafeh, 2002, p. ii)

These findings reinforce the assumption that there is an advantage for students with access to the Internet and qualify the adeptness of the students by referring to them as *Internet-savvy*. This is another important factor in the argument that the students with Internet at home will perform differently because their additional exposure to the Internet will result in greater familiarity with the Internet and hence, more adept usage.

Levin and Arafeh (2002) classified the students in this study as having five different metaphors for describing their use of the Internet for schoolwork: as virtual textbook and reference library, as virtual tutor and study shortcut, as virtual study group, as virtual guidance counselor, and as virtual locker, backpack, and notebook.

Internet Access at Home and Student Use

The next three figures presented, Figure 1, Internet use among children at home / any location, 2001 as a percent of U.S. population; Figure 2, Internet use by age and location, 2001; and Figure 3, Internet use among 10 to 17 year olds by income and location, 2001, are reproduced from the U.S. Department of Commerce. All three of these figures were constructed with data from the National Telecommunications and Information Administration (NTIA) and U.S. Department of Labor Employment Standards Administration (ESA), U.S. Department of Commerce, using U.S. Census Bureau Current Population Survey Supplements.

FIGURE 1.   Internet Use among Children at Home / any Location, 2001 as
a Percent of U.S. Population

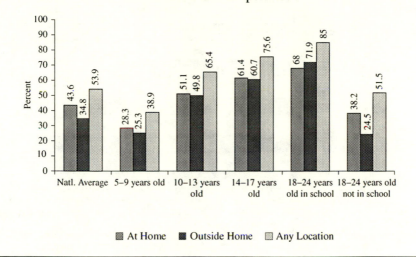

Source: U.S. Department of Commerce, 2002, p. 44.

The data in Figure 1 indicates the younger generations are by far the ones most likely to be using the Internet. The national average for all Internet use has exceeded half of all Americans. The group with the highest use was the 18 to 24 year olds, just beyond the scope of this study. The 10- to 13-year-old group and the 14- to 17-year-old group are the students of concern in this study. Their use of the Internet at home was 55.1% and 61.4%, respectively, in 2001.

Further analysis of the location where the Internet is being used is provided in Figure 2. For the 14 to 17 year olds, most students are using the Internet both at home and at school, 42.8% of the total. This does not hold true to the 10 to 13 year olds, of whom only 32.9% use the Internet both at home and at school. It should be reasonable to question if that has changed since the 2001 publication of this research. Those who used the Internet only in school, 12.8% and 12.6%, respectively, are both smaller groups than those who use the Internet only at home, 18.7% and 18.6%. These two groups, School only and Home only, combined

FIGURE 2.   Internet Use by Age and Location, 2001

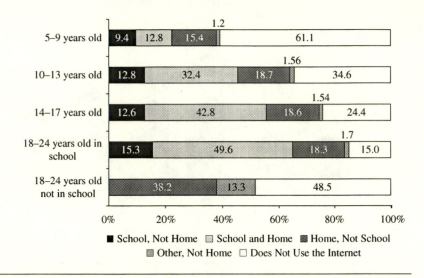

Source: U.S. Department of Commerce, 2002, p. 46.

were smaller than the group of those who were using the Internet both at home and at school already in 2001. Since the publication of the U.S. Department of Commerce report on how Americans made use of the Internet, The Pew Internet & American Life Project published results indicating that more students (94%) are using the Internet (Levin & Arafeh, 2002).

Personal Empowerment in the Study of Home Internet Use by Low-Income Families, conducted by Bier (1997), was structured as an ethnographic study. One of the conclusions in this study was the most disadvantaged participants would become the most enthusiastic users; for example, those who would benefit the most from access to the Internet. In this study, participants who were classified as *information have-nots* were given free Internet access in their homes from December of 1994 until January of 1996. The one-year of Internet access was evaluated and Bier concluded, "The data collected during this study provide strong evidence for the Internet's potential to empower and enrich the lives if those with access" (Conclusion section, ¶ 1). Further,

FIGURE 3. Internet Use among 10 to 17 Year Olds by Income and Location, 2001

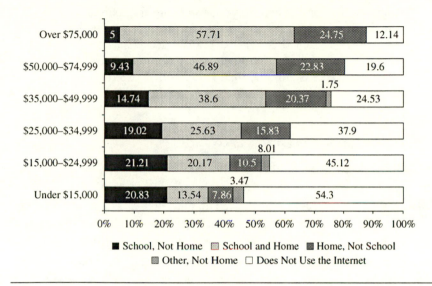

Source: U.S. Department of Commerce, 2002, p. 50.

"Having determined that ideal Internet access can indeed be an effective mechanism through which families from underserved communities may be empowered, we must identify technological and organizational strategies, tools, and models of access that are both effective and practical" (Bier, 1997, Discussion section, ¶ 3). "The ethnographically informed results of this study indicate that home Internet access enabled the research participants to experience powerful emotional and psychological transformations" (Bier, 1997, Discussion section, ¶ 3). These sorts of transformations would support the idea that Internet at home would contribute to a difference in student performance independent of family affluence.

AFFLUENCE EFFECT ON STUDENT PERFORMANCE

The following data from the U.S. Department of Commerce (Figures 1 and 2) appears to indicate that there is an economic difference among those who *have* and *do not have* Internet access. This is notion is summarized

> Surveys for commercial purposes indicate that parents are purchasing computers, software, and Internet connections to provide their children with an "advantage." Consequently, the children from more-advantaged circumstances gain even more access at home than in school. Those from less-advantaged homes are becoming a technological underclass. (Kafai et al., 2002, p. 64)

Household Income and Internet Access

In support of the assertion Kafai et al. put forth, *less-advantaged homes are becoming a technological underclass*, the U.S. Department of Commerce published the data in Figure 3 in 2002. The data suggests there is a relationship among the factors of income and Internet access at home.

A passing examination of Figure 3 reveals a pattern of descending use of the Internet according to the category of income. The group not using the Internet steadily grows with the descending income categories, from 12.14% for those whom earned more than $75,000, 19.6% for those who earned $50,000–$74,999, 24.53% for those who earned $35,000–$49,999, 37.9% for those who earned $25,000–$34,999, 45.12% for those who earned $15,000–$24,999, and 54.3% for those who earned less than $15,000 a year. The pattern is inverted when looking at those who use the Internet both at home and at school with 57.71% for those who earned $75,000, 46.89% for those who earned $50,000–$74,999, 38.6% for those who earned $35,000–$49,999, 25.63% for those who earned $25,000–$34,999, 20.17% for those who earned $15,000–$24,999, and 13.54% for those who earned less than $15,000 a year.

Aside from the question of access, there is also an issue of *how* the resources are used. This question is partially addressed from the results of a data-mining study, Young Children's Access to Computers in the Home and at School in 1999 and 2000, performed by Rathbun et al., published in *Education Statistics Quarterly*. The data was mined from the U.S. Department of Education's National Center for Education Statistics (NCES) from a study performed in 1998 involving more than 22,000 students.

Rathbun et al., offers from the analysis of the data, "… the purposes for which young children used computers at home varied by children's gender, race / ethnicity, and SES [socio-economic-status]. For example, family SES was positively related to children's use of home computers for educational purposes overall" (2003, p. 12). If these results are valid, they may set up a doubling effect of the digital divide. Those who did not have Internet access may not be as likely to have contributed to the advancement of their children's education.

"Who's Wired and Who's Not: Children's Access to and Use of Computer" was published in *The Future of Children* and submitted by Becker (2000). Much of the data he puts forth is from 1998. Although the numbers relating to access are likely to have changed in the years following this study, the activities that students pursue may have followed a trend that was already being indicated in other studies. Becker's study, states the "data suggest that lower-income students use computers more often for repetitive practice, whereas higher-income students use computers more often for more sophisticated, intellectually complex applications" (Becker, 2000, p. 44). This research indicated that these differences in use were school-based. It is unknown if the same results hold true for home-based technology use.

More than half of all American households are now on the Internet (U.S. Department of Commerce, 2002). Most students have Internet access at school, and for those who do not have Internet access at home, "About 11% of these wired teenagers say their primary access to the Internet is at school. Our survey suggests that school is often the place where those who are less privileged have their primary access to the Internet" (Lenhart et al., 2001, p. 3).

Embedded in the income question is the understanding of parental vocation. As it relates to this research, there is evidence that links parent's computer usage at work to usage at home. "The data show that when parents use computers at work, however, they are much more likely to provide their children with access to computers at home, especially those in low-income families" (Becker, 2000, p. 66). This notion is further reinforced: "The presence of someone who uses a computer or the Internet at work in a household is associated with substantially higher computer ownership or Internet use for that household, by a margin of about 77% to 35%" (U.S. Department of Commerce, 2002, p. 2).

Household Income and Academic Standing

It is common to find a statement like *research has shown that test scores closely correlated with a parent's income and educational level*; however, it is not common to find supporting data. The assumption being that greater resources within a given students home will avail a greater variety of experiences. Table 1, Scholastic Assessment Test score averages by Family Income, 1995–1996, 1997–1998, and 1999–2000, reveals the differences in scaled scores. The extreme spread ranges over one hundred points in between the highest and lowest income groups in all categories and years.

Figure 4, Scholastic Assessment Test Score averages by family income, 1995–1996, 1997–1998, and 1999–2000, illustrates the data from Table 1. The trend for those with greater income to have children whom score higher is quite apparent.

Parent Education Level and Academic Standing

Parent's education has also proven to be a factor that appears to be related to academic standing. Figure 5, average student scale score in reading, age 9: Selected years, 1971 to 1999, contains nearly 30 years worth of data. The pattern that emerges is that children whose parents have higher levels of education achieve higher scores on standardized tests. Those children who were raised in households with a parent having post high school education appear to have higher average test scores over the two other categories.

Table 2, Scholastic Assessment Test score averages by parent education, 1995–1996, 1997–1998, and 1999–2000, is the data used to generate Figure 6. The tendency illustrated in the figure and supported by the data in the table supports the notion that greater parent education seems to be related to difference in student test scores.

There appears to be evidence supporting the fact that the education level of parents and student performances are related. Both the effect of the parents' education levels and household income need to be considered in an investigation of the contribution of Internet access to student academic standing. As summarized:

> Of course, student use of the Internet for school does not occur in a vacuum. Students' experiences, and those of their

TABLE 1. Scholastic Assessment Test Score Averages by Family Income, 1995–1996, 1997–1998, and 1999–2000

Selected characteristics	1995–1996			1997–1998			1999–2000		
	Verbal Score	Math Score	%	Verbal Score	Math Score	%	Verbal Score	Math Score	%
All students	505	508	100	505	512	100	505	514	100
Family income									
Less than $10,000	429	444	4	427	446	5	425	447	4
$10,001 to $20,000	456	464	8	451	463	9	447	460	8
$20,001 to $30,000	482	482	10	477	482	11	471	478	10
$30,001 to $40,000	497	495	12	495	497	13	490	493	12
$40,001 to $50,000	509	507	10	506	509	11	503	505	10
$50,001 to $60,000	517	517	9	514	518	11	511	515	11
$60,001 to $70,000	524	525	7	521	525	9	517	522	9
$70,001 to $80,000	531	533	6	527	532	8	524	530	8
$80,001 to $100,000	541	544	7	539	546	9	536	543	10
More than $100,001	560	569	9	559	572	13	558	571	16

Source: National Center for Educational Statistics (2004). *Digest of Statistical Tables and Figures—2003.* Table 135. Scholastic Assessment Test score averages, by selected student characteristics: 1995–1996, 1997–1998, and 1999–2000.

FIGURE 4.   Scholastic Assessment Test Score Averages by Family Income,
1995–1996, 1997–1998, and 1999–2000

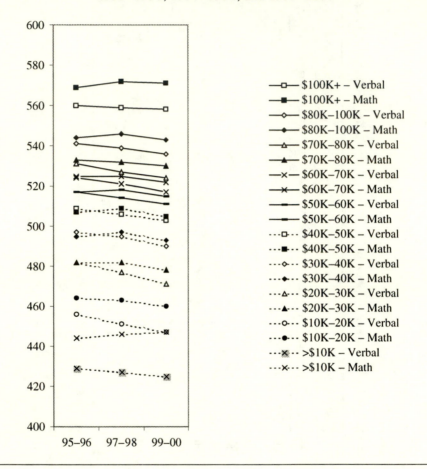

Source: National Center for Educational Statistics (2004). *Digest of Statistical Tables and Figures—2003* Table 135. Scholastic Assessment Test score averages, by selected student characteristics: 1995–1996, 1997–1998, and 1999–2000.

FIGURE 5.   Average Student Scale Score in Reading, Age 9: Selected Years, 1971 to 1999

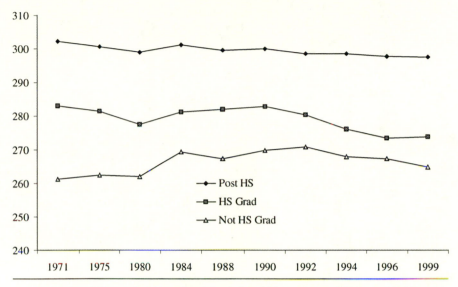

Source: National Center for Educational Statistics (2004). *Digest of Statistical Tables and Figures—2003*. Table 110. Average Student Scale Score in reading, by age and selected student and school characteristics: Selected years, 1971 to 1999.

states, districts, schools, teachers, and parents, strongly affect how the Internet is adopted in schools. Nonetheless, large numbers of students say they are changing because of their out-of-school use of the Internet—and their reliance on it. Internet-savvy students are coming to school with different expectations, different skills, and access to different resources. (Levin & Arafeh, 2002, p. v)

These statements by Levin and Arafeh (2002) reinforce the importance of determining whether the effect of Internet access at home truly operates independently of other established factors.

MEASURES

The measures for this study are survey and standardized test data. The San Miguel GEARUP Partnership requires that parents of participants to

TABLE 2.   Scholastic Assessment Test Score Averages by Parent Education, 1995–1996, 1997–1998, and 1999–2000

Selected characteristics	1995–1996			1997–1998			1999–2000		
	Verbal Score	Math Score	%	Verbal Score	Math Score	%	Verbal Score	Math Score	%
All students	505	508	100	505	512	100	505	514	100
Highest Level of Parental Education									
No High School Diploma	414	439	4	411	441	4	413	442	4
High School Diploma	475	474	31	473	477	34	472	477	33
Associate Degree	489	487	7	489	491	8	488	491	9
Bachelor's Degree	525	529	25	525	532	28	525	533	29
Graduate Degree	556	558	23	556	563	25	558	566	25

Source: National Center for Educational Statistics (2004). *Digest of Statistical Tables and Figures—2003.* Table 135. Scholastic Assessment Test score averages, by selected student characteristics: 1995–1996, 1997–1998, and 1999–2000.

Note: Because of survey item non-response, percentage distributions may not add to 100%.

FIGURE 6. Scholastic Assessment Test Score Averages by Parent Education, 1995–1996, 1997–1998, and 1999–2000

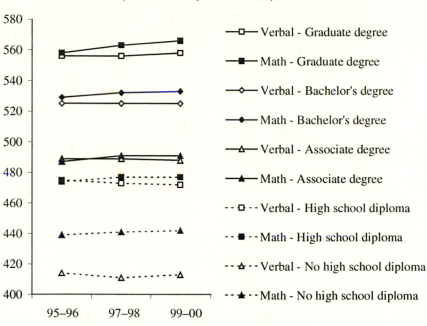

Source: National Center for Educational Statistics (2004). Digest of Statistical Tables and Figures–2003. Table 135. Scholastic Assessment Test score averages, by selected student characteristics: 1995–1996, 1997–1998, and 1999–2000.

complete a survey in the form of an annual application. The standardized test used in New Mexico in 2004 was the CTB / McGraw-Hill–TerraNova. The particular data set to be used from the battery of data available are the NCE total score. This section describes the survey (application form), the standardized test, and the NCE total score.

San Miguel GEARUP Partnership Application Form

Parents of participants complete an application form annually. The Appendix *NMHU / San Miguel GEAR-UP Student Application, 2003–2004 School Year*, contains a reproduction of the survey form. The data collected from this instrument are used to conduct the GEARUP program and complete the Annual Performance Review (APR). There is a high rate of return on the applications because completed applications are required before any students can obtain their earned reward. The participant's application form contains questions that are within the scope of the objectives of GEARUP, for example, Do you plan to go on to college? What college? What major?

For the purposes of this study, three of the San Miguel / New Mexico Highlands University GEARUP Partnership application (survey) questions are relevant: (1) Do you have Internet access? Yes ____No ____, (2) Range of Family Income: ____$0–10,000____$10,000–20,000____$20,000–30,000 ____$30,000–40,000____$40,000–50,000____$50,000–60,000____Above $60,000; and (3) What is the highest level of education that was received by each family member?

NCE Score

Forms of measurement are an important aspect of research. There are many types of results available from standardized tests. NP are perhaps the most common result published in the general media. The NP scale represents a means of arranging the results in order of 1 to 100, without any reference to the difference among those rated on the scale. The Normal-Curve Equivalents (NCE) appears to be similar to the NP score commonly used to describe student performance on standardized test scores because the scores range from 1 to 99. The differences are that the scores are fit to a normal distribution, with a mean of 50, and a standard deviation of 21.06 (Gottfredson, 2004; Gregg, 2004).

> The NCE was developed to allow mathematical manipulation of NP scores—especially for program evaluation and research requiring the comparison of scores across groups or across time. The NCE scores can be thought of as NP scores rescaled on an equal interval scale (which allows them to be used in mathematical calculations such as deriving a mean score). (Indiana Department of Education, Normal Curve Equivalent Score section, 2005, ¶ 1)

As the NCE score has an equal interval scale, it was selected as the score to be used for the analysis of this study. The NCE is a *continuous numeric scale* which is the "highest level of measurement" as defined by Wearden and Dowdy (1991, p. 28). The attributes of the NCE score qualify it as a good selection from the battery of scores produced by standardized tests. The NCE scores will also meet the data distribution assumptions of many statistical analysis methods.

The use of the NCE score will permit students from different grades to be grouped into a single dataset. This is possible because the score is a number ranging in the same domain for each grade. The score reports the academic standing of students relative to their grade level.

The particular score to be used in this research is the NCE total, because the concern is with overall academic standing, not for any particular subject. The NCE Total score is a composite score of Reading, Reading Vocabulary, Language, Language Mechanics, Math, Math Computation, Science, Social Studies, Spelling, and Word Analysis scores.

CTB / McGraw-Hill–TerraNova

CTB / McGraw-Hill has seventy years of experience in producing tests and working with local and state agencies. During the 2003–2004 school year "… education in New Mexico was guided by the State Board's strategic plan, 'Charting Student Success in the New Millennium,' a quality, comprehensive, system-based approach to bring about needed educational reform" (New Mexico Public Education Department, 2004, p. 5). As a consequence, a standardized measure was selected to be used statewide. The selection was for a standardized test; the CTB / McGraw-Hill–TerraNova (CTB / McGraw-Hill, 2004). "Due to concerns over test security, New Mexico for a second year used a new form of the *TerraNova* called *The Second Edition, Complete Battery (CAT)*" (New Mexico Public Education Department, 2004, p. 11). This is the exact form of data upon which this study will be based.

PROGRAM DESCRIPTIONS

The research will use data from the specific population that participates in the NMHU San Miguel GEARUP Partnership. The first section describes the GEARUP program, as it is offered from the U.S. Department of Education.

The second section describes the San Miguel GEARUP Partnership. The final section describes the database the San Miguel GEARUP Partnership utilizes to conduct program activities.

GEARUP

Gaining Early Awareness and Readiness for Undergraduate Programs (GEARUP) is a federally funded program. The GEARUP Program is funded at over $300 million annually and serves over 1.2 million students nationally. GEARUP has received almost $1.2 billion since its creation and has 280 partnership grants and 36 state grants (NCCEP, 2005).

> The GEARUP program is a discretionary grant program designed to increase the number of low-income students who are prepared to enter and succeed in postsecondary education. GEARUP provides five-year grants to states and partnerships to provide services at high-poverty middle and high schools. GEARUP grantees serve an entire cohort of students beginning no later than the seventh grade and follow the cohort through high school. GEARUP funds are also used to provide college scholarships to low-income students. (U.S. Department of Education, Purpose section, 2005, ¶ 1)

San Miguel GEARUP Partnership

The San Miguel GEARUP Partnership was conducted in Las Vegas, New Mexico, at New Mexico Highlands University. There are two school districts, a community college and a university participating in the partnership. The participants are: Las Vegas City Schools, West Las Vegas Schools, Luna Community College, and New Mexico Highlands University. This partnership was funded by the U.S. Department of Education for five years, from 2000 to 2005.

The partnership objectives were to improve academic performance of the participating students in two major ways: first, by enabling individualized curriculum for students in reading comprehension and math, and second, a student incentive system. Individualized curriculums are supported such as SRA reading kits, along with Renaissance Learning products, such as

Accelerated Math and Accelerated Reading. In the students incentive system, students "earn points for completing their educational tasks, for participating in the management of the system, and for demonstrating positive social behavior. Points are used for rewards such as monthly field trips" (U.S. Department of Education, 2004, p. 91). Over 3500 students have interacted with this GEARUP program since 2000.

NMHU / GEARUP Database

The San Miguel GEARUP Partnership has developed a database containing the program information necessary to conduct the initiatives set forth by the U.S. Department of Education and the program goals of the San Miguel GEARUP Partnership. The database has evolved from a series of spreadsheets, to a Microsoft Access relational database and its current state as a fully normalized MS-SQL 2000 database. The primary sources of data in the database are demographics collected from participant parents (Appendix A), academic and behavioral data entered by teachers, and imported data. Imported data sources include results of standardized tests, state content standards and benchmarks, and educational objectives.

The system maintains internal integrity by the use of a GUID. A GUID is a unique 128-bit number that is produced by the Windows OS or by some Windows applications to identify a particular component, application, file, database entry, and / or user (Webopedia, 2004). These unique identifiers meet all the criteria for a relational database to have integrity at a table level, database level, and entire systems level (Hernandez, 2003, pp. 261–265). The GUID is designed to be unique across all systems and lends a high degree of certainty that a record referred to in any data set is indeed the record called or requested.

PRIOR AND RELATED RESEARCH

Previous research has indicated a strong need for more studies like this one conducted. Most research on Internet and public education has been a count of network connections, machines and an accounting of the bandwidth available to how count of how many students. Other kinds of research included ones which studied how may students *have* access within the schools.

> the major emphasis of educational technology research-
> ers has been the development and use of educational
> technologies within school settings. Noticeably absent
> has been research and considerations that focus on the
> home as a computer-based learning environment and
> potential connections between school and home learning.
> (Kafai et al., 2002, p. 52)

Furthermore the research focusing on computers within the home is becoming quickly dated, because the issues cited in the conclusions of research from ten and more years ago has questionable validity considering the vast improvements in current computer and Internet technologies. In 1995, Internet connections were rare and had very limited value. Research from five years ago may be questioned as the nature of distributed applications has undergone several technical evolutions.

Prior Research

The findings by Attewell and Battle (1999) support the premises of this research. Their findings indicate there exist relationships between the factors of home computer access and higher test scores in the National Educational Longitudinal Study of 1988.

> We find that having a home computer is associated with
> higher test scores in mathematics and reading, even after
> controlling for family income, and for cultural and social
> capital. However, children from high socioeconomic status
> homes achieve larger educational gains from home comput-
> ers than lower SES children. Boys' performance advantage
> is larger than girls'. Ethnic minorities gain far less of
> a performance boost than whites. Home computing may
> generate another "Sesame Street Effect" whereby an innova-
> tion which held great promise for poorer children to catch
> up educationally with more affluent children, in practice is
> increasing the educational gap between affluent and poor,
> between boys and girls, between ethnic minorities and
> whites, even among those with access to the technology.
> (Attewell & Battle, 1999, p. 1)

There are two notable issues arising from the data analyzed in this study. First, there was some degree of effect where socioeconomic-status was concerned. Second, the data from 1988 which were analyzed eleven years later in 1999 may not be valid. Even by Attewell and Battle's assessment, the nature of the technology—home computers for their study—had changed, and may have an impact on the results of a similar study. The research is of interest because the design is comprehensive in the treatment of other factors that may contribute to differences in student performance. This approach supports the rationale of the design of this study by giving consideration to confounding factors.

> It would be simple to test whether the existence of home computing, by itself, was associated with higher test scores, but that could be misleading. Many factors, from family income to state of residence, are also related to children's academic performance, and some of these are correlated with ownership of a home computer as well. One therefore needs to separate the effects of these multiple determinants of educational performance, and assess the contribution (if any) of home computers net of these other variables. (Attewell & Battle, 1999, p. 3)

A September 2004 publication, *Technology and Equity in Schooling: Deconstructing the Digital Divide*, questions the contribution of technology access in the home, "Although home access to computers has long been regarded as important for supporting students' academic achievement, research suggests that home ownership of computers alone does not level out inequalities in terms of technology's contributions to student learning" (Warschauer & Knobel, 2004, p. 563). What is suggested is that there are other factors beyond ownership, such as the parent setting an example of *what* function, or role, the technology fills. In some cases where a parent is an Internet user at work, the observing child interprets the technology as a tool of work. While in other cases, the child observes Internet use only for entertainment and consequently, perceives the technology as such. This trend is also seen to follow the various income categories.

> Just as children in families with lower income and less-educated parents were much less likely to have a computer in their home—or, if they had a computer, to have one with many features—such children were also less likely to use their family's computer in various ways. (Becker, 2000, p. 63)

In reference to *various ways* Becker (2000) wrote contextually about the use of six applications such as word processors and other productivity technologies typically used outside the educational environment. If one or both parents use these technologies in the workplace, their children were more likely to use these technologies to support learning and completing schoolwork.

Related Study Research

Queries of the West Virginia University Dissertation Database (Dissertation Abstracts Online—OCLC) produced a number of related studies. Some of the results, especially those more than five years old, may no longer reflect the state of Internet usage within the home. However, others reveal results relevant to the aims of this study.

Dissertation research performed by Nonnamaker (2000), *Pre-college Internet use and freshman year academic achievement in a private college: The effect of sociodemographic characteristics, family socioeconomic status, academic ability and high school experiences*, at Fordham University, focused on the assumption that Internet technology will enhance academic achievement in college during the freshman year. Data was collected from the 1998 Student Information Form and included linked grades data from the institution. Findings indicated that "For freshmen grades in the top third of their class, however, both school based and home based pre-college Internet use directly affected academic achievement with home based use enhancing academic achievement, while school based use was, unexpectedly, negative" (Nonnamaker, 2000, ¶ 3). These results support this research as Nonnamaker found that "Internet use directly affected academic achievement" (2000, ¶ 3).

Dissertation research performed by Davis (2003), *An investigation of parental perceptions of and attitudes toward computer use in two predominantly Hispanic communities in the southwestern border region*, at

New Mexico State University, focused on parental perceptions of and attitudes toward their children's computer use. Data was collected from discussions with 26 participants in five parent focus groups. "Qualitative research analysis techniques were used to triangulate discussions" (Davis, 2003, ¶ 2). Four themes emerged in this research: "(a) digital divide issues, (b) the desires of respondents from all socioeconomic groups for technology training, (c) respondents' fears to use the Internet, and (d) respondents' concerns about children spending too much time on computers" (Davis, 2003, ¶ 3). Additional results included concerns about poverty stricken parents not being able to afford computers and that parents lacked experience to understand what their children are learning. "Parents from all ethnic backgrounds and income levels expressed the desire to have free computer training" (Davis, 2003, ¶ 4). Finally, the "digital divide problem was not an ethnic issue; rather, it was a socioeconomic status issue" (Davis, 2003, ¶ 4). These results support this research because Davis states that "it was a socioeconomic status issue" (Davis, 2003, ¶ 4), thereby supporting the importance of the confounding factors of this study.

Dissertation research performed by Toriskie (1999), *The Effects of Internet Usage on Student Achievement and Student Attitudes* (*Fourth-Grade, Social Studies*), at Loyola University of Chicago, focused on whether or not the use of the Internet would affect student achievement in social studies or students' attitudes toward school. Data was collected using the Social Studies Battery of the California Achievement Test and a Student Attitude Survey. The variables in this study were gender, ethnicity, socioeconomic status, and home use of the Internet. "Internet usage was found to have a positive impact on both student achievement in social studies and on student attitudes" (Toriskie, 1999, ¶ 3). These findings support this research since differences in academic standing were attributed to Internet usage.

RESEARCH METHOD

> *Interpreting statistics is an art—an art of making judgments under uncertainty.* But as it becomes easier to obtain statistics on much larger samples, and as the providers of statistics become more professional, the problem of error is reduced and the problem of spurious associations remains.

> As the quality and quantity of data obtained in an observational study increases, the problem of confounding becomes the central problem. (Schield, 1999, p. 5)

To dismiss confounding factors can cause a spurious association. "What we take into account (or fail to take into account) strongly influences the conclusions we reach" (Schield, 1999, p. 5). According to Schield, the three means of avoiding a spurious association are to (1) increase the sample size, (2) eliminate the problem of bias, and (3) eliminate the influence of confounding factors. To determine if there is a difference in academic standing for those whom have Internet access at home, consideration of other factors need to be included in the research design. The research design should determine differences, and potential interactions among factors such as Internet access at home, family affluence, and academic achievement.

The three-way factorial Analysis of Variance (ANOVA) can be used when an "investigator is interested in the combined effect" (Wearden, 1991, p. 397) of the factors. "Factorial arrangements allow us to study the *interaction* between two or more factors" (Horsley, 2004, p. 1). The results of this method produce main effects and interaction effects. In essence, this method of analysis can be used to test for differences among the means of the factors and the means of the various combinations interactions.

CHAPTER THREE

METHOD

DESIGN

The purpose of this study was to investigate differences in academic standing among those with Internet access at home and those without Internet access, and if the potential academic standing differences are dependent or independent of family affluence. A quasi-experimental research design was employed to determine if there were differences due to these factors. The statistical method of three-way factorial ANOVA (A × B × C Factorial Design) was used for analysis.

This was a post hoc quasi-experimental design because the independent variables were not randomly assigned to the participants and the data were based upon what has already occurred (survey results from the 2003–2004 school year, and test scores from the Spring 2004). The selection of a three-way factorial ANOVA was supported because it would indicate if interactions among the factors existed. Post hoc comparisons and / or post hoc analyses were conducted if significant differences were determined to exist.

Research Question

What are the differences among the standardized test scores of students due to factors of Internet access at home, household income, and the highest level of education attained by mother, father, or guardian?

Independent Variables

The independent variables in this study were (1) Internet access at home, (2) family income, and (3) highest level of education attained by mother, father, or guardian. The independent variables were gathered from responses on the San Miguel GEARUP Partnership application. On the application, parents indicate whether or not the students have Internet access at home. Parents of participants also mark the form to indicate their household income and the level of education attained by mother, father, and / or guardian. The highest level of education achieved was selected. To summarize, the independent variables were:

- Internet access at home, that were grouped: (yes vs. no)
- Family income, that may have been grouped in an arrangement such as: ($1–$20,000, $20,001–$30,000, $30,001–$50,000, and $50,001 +)
- Highest level of education attained by mother, father, or guardian, that may have been grouped in an arrangement such as: (elementary school—high school, some college—2-year degree, 4-year degree, and graduate degree)

The definitions of categories were dependent upon the data. The particular groupings of both family income and highest level of education attained by mother, father, or guardian were determined by analyzing the data.

Dependent Variable

In this study, the dependent variable was the Normal-Curve Equivalents (NCE) total test score as calculated by the CTB / McGraw-Hill–TerraNova. The NCE Total score is a composite score of Reading, Reading Vocabulary, Language, Language Mechanics, Math, Math Computation, Science, Social Studies, Spelling, and Word Analysis scores. The NCE score fits a normally distributed curve, and the data should meet the assumptions for the method of analysis. To summarize, the dependent variable is:

> NCE Total score from the CTB / McGraw-Hill– TerraNova NCE

Factorial ANOVA

For the research question, a three-way factorial ANOVA was chosen to determine which factor had the most effect on the dependent variable, the NCE test scores, and to examine the degree of interaction among the independent variables (Wearden & Dowdy, 1991, p. 409). Table 3, Quasi-Experimental Research Design: Three-Way ANOVA—2 × 4 × 4 Factorial ANOVA, illustrates how the independent variables, and the dependent variable, represented by the *xx*, may have been structured.

The exact form ($a \times b \times c$) of the factorial ANOVA was determined by the data. It was likely to be smaller than the example provided, and the category groupings were different. Certain categories were collapsed together to ensure adequate data in each cell of the table. For instance, if inadequate data were available for households led by high-school graduates whom are earning $50,001+, that column would be combined with the next lower category to obtain an adequate number of data sets. Likewise, highest level of education within the household would also require the collapsing of rows to ensure adequate data in each cell.

Hypothesis Statement

Null Hypothesis

Because neither the size (number of rows and columns) nor particular groupings of the three-way ANOVA are known until the data was analyzed, the precise form of the null hypothesis was speculation. Assuming the grouping would take the form illustrated in Table 3, the null hypothesis would be:

> There is no significant difference, at the alpha = 0.05 level, for the effects of the Independent Variables of (A) Internet access at home (yes vs. no) by (B) family income ($1–$20,000, $20,001–$30,000, $30,001–$50,000, $50,001+) by (C) highest level of education attained by mother or father, or guardian

TABLE 3.   Quasi-Experimental Research Design: Three-Way ANOVA—2 × 4 × 4 Factorial ANOVA

	FACTOR A: Internet Access at Home							
	YES				NO			
FACTOR B: Household Income	$0–$20K	$20K–$30K	$30K–$50K	$50K+	$0–$20K	$20K–$30K	$30K–$50K	$50K+
FACTOR C: Highest Level of Education Attained by Mother, Father or Guardian								
Elementary School—High School	xx	xx	xx	xx	xx	xx	xx	xx
Some College—2-Year Degree	xx	xx	xx	xx	xx	xx	xx	xx
4-Year Degree	xx	xx	xx	xx	xx	xx	xx	xx
Graduate Degree	xx	xx	xx	xx	xx	xx	xx	xx

Source: Dependent Variable: Spring 2004 CTB / McGraw-Hill–TerraNova NCE Total Test score.

(elementary school—high school, some college—2-year degree, 4-year degree, and graduate degree) on the dependent variable (NCE Total score).

The null hypothesis states the means of all groups would be equal. Expressed mathematically in simplest form:

$$\mu_{oA} = \mu_{oB} = \mu_{oC} = \mu_{oAB} = \mu_{oAC} = \mu_{oBC} = \mu_{oABC}$$

The full expression of null hypothesis states that all means within groups as well as among groups will be equal. Using Table 3 as a reference, all means within and among combinations of cells will be equal. Expressed mathematically:

Main effect A: $\mu_{\text{Internet (yes)}} = \mu_{\text{Internet (no)}}$

Main effect B: $\mu_{\text{income (\$1–\$20,000)}} = \mu_{\text{income (\$20,001–\$30,000)}}$
$= \mu_{\text{income (\$30,001–\$50,000)}} = \mu_{\text{income (\$50,001+)}}$

Main effect C: $\mu_{\text{education (elementary school to high school)}}$
$= \mu_{\text{education (some college—2-year degree)}} = \mu_{\text{education (4-year degree)}}$
$= \mu_{\text{education (graduate degree)}}$

Interaction AB: $\mu_{\text{Internet (yes) income (\$1–\$20,000)}}$
$= \mu_{\text{Internet (yes) income (\$20,001–\$30,000)}}$
$= \mu_{\text{Internet (yes) income (\$30,001–\$50,000)}} = \mu_{\text{Internet (yes) income (\$50,001+)}}$
$= \mu_{\text{Internet (no) income (\$1–\$20,000)}} = \mu_{\text{Internet (no) income (\$20,001–\$30,000)}}$
$= \mu_{\text{Internet (no) income (\$30,001–\$50,000)}} = \mu_{\text{Internet (no) income (\$50,001+)}}$

Interaction AC: $\mu_{\text{Internet (yes) education (elementary school–high school)}}$
$= \mu_{\text{Internet (yes) education (some college—2-year degree)}}$
$= \ldots = \mu_{\text{Internet (no) education (some college—2-year degree)}}$
$= \mu_{\text{Internet (no) education (4-year degree)}} = \mu_{\text{Internet (no) education (graduate degree)}}$

Interaction BC: $\mu_{\text{income (\$1–\$20,000) education (elementary school–high school)}}$
$= \mu_{\text{income (\$1–\$20,000) education (some college—2-year degree)}}$
$= \ldots = \mu_{\text{income (\$50,001+) education (some college—2-year degree)}}$
$= \mu_{\text{income (\$50,001+) education (4-year degree)}}$
$= \mu_{\text{income (\$50,001+) education (graduate degree)}}$

Interaction ABC:

$\mu_{\text{Internet (yes) income (\$1–\$20,000) education (elementary school–high school)}}$

$= \mu_{\text{Internet (yes) income (\$1–\$20,000) education (some college—2-year degree)}}$

$= \cdots = \mu_{\text{Internet (no) income (\$50,001+) education (4-year degree)}}$

$= \mu_{\text{Internet (no) income (\$50,001+) education (graduate degree)}}$

The means (yes vs. no) of the main effect A (Internet access at home) will be equal. The means ($1–$20,000, $20,001–$30,000, $30,001–$50,000, and $50,001+) of the main effect B (income) will be equal. The means (elementary school–high school, some college—2-year degree, 4-year degree, and graduate degree) of the main effect C (highest level of attained education) will be equal. The means of the 8 combinations of the interaction effect AB (Internet and income) will be equal. The means of the 8 combinations of the interaction effect AC (Internet and Education) will be equal. The means of the 16 combinations of the interaction effect BC (income and education) will be equal. Finally, the means of all 32 combinations of Internet, income and education of the interaction effect ABC will be equal.

Instruments

Data for this study are from two sources:

1. Survey: NMHU / GEARUP program application, and
2. Test score: NCE total score from the CTB / McGraw-Hill–TerraNova standardized test.

The NMHU / GEARUP program application was adapted from an application used by the Yakima, WA GEARUP program and developed with assistance from the University of Washington. The San Miguel GEARUP Partnership maintains a large database of participant demographics and student performance data. This database contains the data required to perform a statistical analysis of the proposed relationship of Internet access at home and academic standing. The NMHU / GEARUP database was queried for necessary data:

- Internet at home
- Household income
- Highest level of education attained by mother, father, or guardian
- Spring 2004 standardized test scores (NCE Total score)

The determination of Internet access at home, income, and education level of parents or guardians was self-reported on the annual NMHU / GEARUP application. These responses were coded into the NMHU / GEARUP database.

The standardized test scores were from the CTB / McGraw-Hill–TerraNova, Second Edition, Complete Battery (CAT). The score used in this research was the NCE total which was a composite score of Reading, Reading Vocabulary, Language, Language Mechanics, Math, Math Computation, Science, Social Studies, Spelling, and Word Analysis scores. The NCE score is similar to the NP, however, the NCE scores are equal interval and fit to a normal distribution.

Matrix of Analysis

Table 4, Matrix of Analysis, is a depiction of the data sources and analysis required for answering the research question. The first column illustrates the

TABLE 4.   Matrix of Analysis

Independent Variables	Data Source	Proposed Analysis
Internet at home	Survey (NMHU / GEARUP applications)	A × B × C ANOVA
Household income		
Highest level of education attained by mother, father, or guardian		
Dependent Variable	**Data Source**	**Proposed Analysis**
NCE Total test Score	Standardized test scores (CTB / McGraw-Hill–Terra Nova)	A × B × C ANOVA

independent variables and dependent variable of the study. The independent variables were Internet access at home, household income, and the highest level of education attained by mother, father, or guardian. The dependent variable was the NCE total score. The Data Sources Column illustrates the two sources of data for this research—survey data and the results of the standardized test scores. The Proposed Analysis indicates the method of a three-way ANOVA.

Population and Sample

The population of this study was from two school districts within San Miguel County in northern New Mexico. This population was comprised of households with students who were in grades six to ten in the 2003–2004 school years. These two school districts were primarily Hispanic (85%), and more than 80% of the student population was receiving free / reduced in school lunch.

Parents of students participating in the San Miguel GEARUP Partnership were required to submit an annual application for their children to participate in the GEARUP program. In excess of 95% of the households in these two school districts completed the application. A great number of complete datasets existed within the 1963 applications received in the 2003–2004 school year. A complete dataset was a result of a union of all the variables in the study: Internet access at home (yes vs. no), family income ($1–$20,000, $21,000–$30,000, $30,001–$50,001, $50,001+) at least one education level of the mother, father, or guardian (single highest will be selected), and the standardized test score (NCE Total of the CTB / McGraw-Hill–TerraNova). Only complete datasets were used.

Although the investigator had particular categories he wished to utilize for the independent variables, the availability of data in particular categorical levels may necessitate modifying the categories. The distribution was shaped by the requirements to provide enough data to place all the cells the A × B × C ANOVA. Certain cells, such as the income of $50,001+ lead by a high-school education head of household would be difficult to populate with an adequate amount of data. The exact shape (number of rows and columns) of the three-way ANOVA would be determined by the distribution of the data.

Human Subjects Clearance

Data queried from the NMHU / GEARUP database did not contain information that could link any particular data set to an individual. Anonymity of participants was guarded and respected. Additionally, permission to use data provided on the NMHU / GEARUP application was provided and released by a guardian signature on the application. The two school districts included in this study had provided permission to use data on the standardized tests. Anonymity was further guaranteed by queries of the NMHU / GEARUP database were based upon the use of GUIDs as the primary keys. The GUIDs will be replaced with a sequence of unrelated numbers (e.g., 1, 2, 3) to further ensure no particular dataset could be related to any particular participant.

PROCEDURE OF ANALYSIS

1. Identified the test for this study as a three-way ANOVA;
2. Designed the A × B × C Factorial ANOVA and set significance levels;
3. Queried the San Miguel GEARUP Partnership database for the data to perform the tests;
4. Formatted and entered data into SPSS in the following form as shown in Table 5;
5. Conducted ANOVA with SPSS;
6. Tested to ensure assumptions of ANOVA are met;

TABLE 5.   Sample of Data for Entry into SPSS

ID ###	Internet Access at Home (0 or 1)	Household Income (1, 2, 3, or 4)	Highest Attained Education in Family (1, 2, 3, or 4)	NCE Total Score (1–99)
1	1	4	3	55
2	0	1	2	47
3	1	3	2	61
N	A	B	C	xx

7. On significant F-test results, performed Scheffé's post hoc analysis;
8. Specified which main effects and / or interaction(s) were significant by reporting multiple comparisons;
9. Presented conclusions from analysis; and
10. Presented findings, conclusions, and recommendations.

CHAPTER FOUR

FINDINGS

This chapter presents findings from the analysis of data to address the research question: What are the differences among the standardized test scores of students related to factors of Internet access at home, household income, and the highest level of education attained by mother, father, or guardian? The first section is a brief discussion of the use of the General Linear Model. This is followed by an explanation of the data used in the analysis. Details will examine the distribution of the data, and the arrangement established for the factorial analyses. The assumptions for an ANOVA are tested. Results of analysis are presented in the order of the portions of the null hypothesis; for example, main effects and interaction effects. Measures of association are presented. Other analyses are presented because these results present interesting implications on findings; which will be addressed in Chapter Five. Four analyses, other than the primary analysis on the full dataset, were performed on trimmed datasets: (1) an unbalanced factorial ANOVA, (2) one-way ANOVA performed on main effects, (3) a completely crossed and balanced factorial ANOVA on a severely reduced data set, and (4) one-way ANOVA on main effects performed with the fully crossed and balanced reduced data set. Finally, this chapter closes with a summary of analyses.

USE OF THE GENERAL LINEAR MODEL

The ANOVA, both factorial and one-way, used the General Linear Model (GLM). The GLM is selected because the data are arranged in categories. The method is essentially a form of regression, evaluating the distance from an "expected mean"; however, the expected mean is not based upon the slope of a "$y = mx + b$" sort of line. Instead of determining the "expected value" of y from the x-position, the expected value of y is determined by the mean of the category to which the value is assigned. If it were displayed on a Cartesian coordinate system, the y-axis is a continuous variable, however, the x-axis of data is on a non-continuous scale, due to the data being based upon categorical groupings, as opposed to a continuous scale.

DATA EXPLANATION

The San Miguel GEARUP Database was queried, and produced 572 complete sets of data. The number of complete sets was lower than expected because the selection of a dataset is based upon the *highest* attained education per household, prior estimates included all education values (up to three per student). The next sections detail how the data distribution was examined to determine the best arrangement for the method of analysis.

Data Queries

The queries were performed in several steps. First, each factor (Internet, income, and education) was queried. These queries used data from the demographics cluster (a set of related vertically integrated tables) and the students table. The results of these three queries were imported into MS Access as separate tables; the native format for the GEARUP archives of standardized test scores. The imported tables were related to the standardized test data and queried for final set results used in the analysis.

The first query was performed to obtain data on Internet access at home. The Structured Query Language (SQL) statement used is shown in Appendix B—Internet Access Query. The second query was performed to obtain data on income levels. The SQL statement used is shown in Appendix C—Income Query. The third query was performed to obtain data on parent /guardian education levels. The SQL statement used is shown in

Appendix D—Education Query. The results of these three queries were imported into MS Access. The standardized test data were related to the three imported tables. Appendix E—NCE Test Scores reveals the SQL statement used to generate a result with data in four fields: Internet, income, education, and NCE score. The final steps to transform the data format for import to SPSS were performed in MS Excel.

Implications of Data Distribution

The method designated for analysis of data was a factorial ANOVA. The challenge inherent in using the factorial was to arrange for a "completely crossed" design (Hays, 1988, p. 430) where every cell in the matrix contains values. A balanced design also contains an equal n, or number of datasets in each cell. Hays stated a strong preference for arranging data in a *completely crossed and balanced* arrangement.

The results of the queries distribution are shown in Table 6, Distribution of data—Internet access at home, and Table 7, Distribution of data—No Internet access at home. Many of the possible combinations were eliminated because of cells that contain no data. This required combing rows and columns of data to obtain an adequate number of test scores for each cell of the factorial ANOVA.

Examination of the data in Tables 6 and 7 revealed certain categories lacked data, most notably on the extremes. For instance, the combination of high income, low education and those without Internet is particularly vacuous. The other area of Tables 6 and 7 that lacked data were the combination those with higher education and lower incomes. Other distribution issues are split among those with and without Internet access. Such is the case of lowest income category with Internet (13) versus the lowest income category without Internet access (75). The lack of data in these cells necessitated the combining of cells for analyses.

Forming Data for Analysis

With 13 of the cells in Tables 6 and 7 containing zeros, i.e. no data, collapsing categories became necessary to form a "completely crossed" design (Hays, 1988, p. 430) where every cell contains values. Given that each cell does not have an equal number of observations, the design is not

TABLE 6. Distribution of Data—Internet Access at Home

Total of Those with Internet Access at Home   276

	Sum	0–10K	10–20K	20–30K	30–40K	40–50K	50–60K	60K+
Sum		13	48	62	32	56	17	48
Finished Elementary School	3	0	1	0	0	2	0	0
Graduated from High School	35	5	11	9	6	3	1	0
Attended College or Training after High School	44	4	8	8	1	16	4	3
Completed a 2-Year College or Training Program	51	1	8	21	6	10	1	4
Completed a 4-Year College or University Degree	58	0	17	10	5	11	5	10
Attended / Completed College Graduate Program	85	3	3	14	14	14	6	31

Note: The dashed lines illustrate the grouping of data.

TABLE 7. Distribution of Data—No Internet Access at Home

Total of Those with No Internet Access at Home　296

	Sum	0–10K	10–20K	20–30K	30–40K	40–50K	50–60K	60K+
Sum		75	74	70	22	18	17	20
Finished Elementary School	9	5	2	1	1	0	0	0
Graduated from High School	64	28	18	13	4	1	0	0
Attended College or Training After High School	76	25	27	14	4	4	0	2
Completed a 2-Year College or Training Program	51	8	11	23	1	3	4	1
Completed a 4-Year College or University Degree	42	4	7	9	4	7	3	8
Attended / Completed College Graduate Program	54	5	9	10	8	3	10	9

Note: The dashed lines illustrate the grouping of data.

balanced. Therefore, the design was completely crossed, and unbalanced. Table 8, Distribution of data—Count of data in each cell, illustrates the number of datasets in each cell of the factorial ANOVA arrangement used to analyze that data. The Group without Internet access and with the lowest income and education is the largest cell with 124 datasets. In an attempt to maintain at least 20 observations per cell, the following grouping was derived.

The distribution was arranged according to the dashed rectangles that group cells in Tables 6 and 7. The n for each cell is shown in Table 9, Distribution of Data for Main Effects. The categories for Effect A (Internet access) were Yes versus No. Effect A has a distribution of 276 for those with Internet versus 296 for those without Internet access. The three categories for Effect B (Income) were: (1) $0–$20K, (2) $20K–$30K, and (3) $30k+. Effect B has a distribution of 210 for those in the lowest income, 132 for those in the second category, and 230 for the third category. The two categories for Effect C (education) essentially were divided by those with/without a 4-year degree. The specific categories for Effect C were: (1) elementary school–high school, some college—2-year degree, and; (2) 4-year degree—graduate program. Effect C has a distribution of 333 for those with lowest education level and 239 for those with highest education level.

Testing the Assumptions for ANOVA

Having obtained results, tests were performed to ensure the data met the assumptions for ANOVA. The next three sections address the testing of

TABLE 8.   Distribution of Data—Count of Data in each Cell

	Internet Access			No Internet Access		
	$0–$20K	$20–$30K	$30k+	$0–$20K	$20–$30K	$30k+
Elementary School—High School, Some College—2-Year Degree	38	38	57	124	51	25
4-Year Degree—Graduate Program	23	24	96	25	19	52

Table 9. Distribution of Data for Main Effects

Effect	Category	n
Effect A—Internet Access at Home	1	276
Effect A—No Internet Access at Home	0	296
Effect B—$0–$20,000	1	210
Effect B—$20,001–$30,000	2	132
Effect B—$30,001+	3	230
Effect C—2-Year Degree or Less	1	333
Effect C—Bachelor's Degree or Greater	2	239

these assumptions in detail. There are three assumptions for an ANOVA (Wearden, 1991, p. 347). These assumptions are:

1. Normality
2. Homoscedasticity (groups have equal variance)
3. Random assignment.

Assumption of Normality

The initial step in this process was to generate a histogram on the data. Figure 7, Histogram of NCE scores illustrates a distribution that is generally unimodal, symmetrical, asymptotic to the *y*-axis, and bell shaped (Wearden, 1991, p. 163). Wearden (1991) states that more than 99% of the distribution should dwell between (3 standard deviations of the mean were calculated (p. 163). The Mean for the NCE on the entire distribution is 46.52 and the standard deviation is 16.02. The range established within 3 standard deviations is 3.13 to 94.58. The number of observations within the range of 3.13 and 94.58 is 569 of the 572 total observations. The result of 569/572 indicates that 99.48% of the observations are within three standard deviations of the mean. Given the results of this test and the histogram, it was concluded that the distribution is relatively normal.

Assumption of Homoscedasticity

Homoscedasticity, equal variance among the groups, can be tested in various ways. A suitable test is Levene's test of homogeneity of variance, which is computed by SPSS to test the ANOVA assumption that each group (category) of the independent)(s) has the same variance …. Note, however, that failure to meet the assumption of homogeneity of variances is not fatal to ANOVA, which is relatively robust, particularly when groups are of equal sample size (Garson, 2005, Assumptions section, ¶ 3).

"When the results of this test are significant, that is, the "2-tail Sig." is less than 0.05, the assumption has been violated" (Wielkiewicz, 2005, Analysis of Variance with SPSS section, ¶ 4). This test produced a significance result of $p = 0.063$. This was greater than the required 0.05, therefore the assumption of homogeneity was valid ($F11, 560 = 1.732$). Full results of this analysis are available in Appendix F—Primary Factorial ANOVA.

Assumption of Random Assignment

This was a post hoc quasi-experimental design because the independent variables were not being randomly assigned to the participants and the data were based upon what has already occurred (survey results from the 2003–2004 school year, and test scores from the Spring 2004). This assumption was violated by the nature of the method.

FIGURE 7. HISTOGRAM OF NCE SCORES

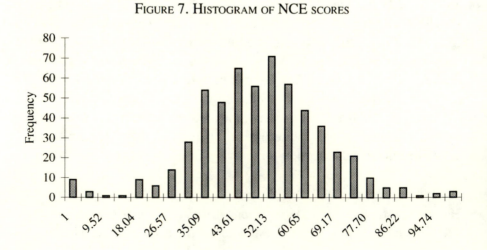

RESULTS OF ANALYSIS

The Null Hypothesis states the means of each row, column and interaction (combination of cells) will be equal. Expressed mathematically:

$$\mu_{oA} = \mu_{oB} = \mu_{oC} = \mu_{oAB} = \mu_{oAC} = \mu_{oBC} = \mu_{oABC}$$

Although a single statement, it essentially was arranged into two broad categories, main effects and interaction effects. Within the main effects, there were three basic statements, and four combinations of interaction effects. Main effects null hypotheses for the distribution is expressed mathematically:

Main effect A: $\mu_{\text{Internet (yes)}} = \mu_{\text{Internet (no)}}$

Main effect B: $\mu_{\text{income (\$1–\$20,000)}} = \mu_{\text{income (\$20,001–\$30,000)}} = \mu_{\text{income (\$30,001+)}}$

Main effect C: $\mu_{\text{education (elementary school–high school–some college—2-year degree)}}$
$= \mu_{\text{education (4 year degree—graduate degree)}}$

Interaction effects null hypotheses for the distribution expressed mathematically:

Interaction AB: $\mu_{\text{Internet (yes) income (\$1–\$20,000)}}$
$= \mu_{\text{Internet (yes) income (\$20,001–\$30,000)}} = \mu_{\text{Internet (yes) income (\$30,001+)}}$
$= \dots = \mu_{\text{Internet (no) income (\$20,001–\$30,000)}} = \mu_{\text{Internet (no) income (\$30,001+)}}$

Interaction AC:

$\mu_{\text{Internet (yes) education (elementary school–high school–some college–2-year degree)}}$
$= \dots = \mu_{\text{Internet (no) education (4 year degree—graduate degree)}}$

Interaction BC:

$\mu_{\text{income (\$1–\$20,000) education (elementary school–high school–some college–2-year degree)}}$
$= \dots = \mu_{\text{income (\$30,001+) education (4 year degree—graduate degree)}}$

Interaction ABC:

$\mu_{\text{Internet (yes) income (\$1–\$20,000) education (elementary school–high school–some college–2-year degree)}} = \dots = \mu_{\text{Internet (no) income (\$30,001+) education (4 year degree—graduate degree)}}$

Main Effects

The results of each of the three main effects are briefly presented. Results presented on each main effect are: means, levels of significance, and post hoc comparisons if the results proved to be significant.

Main Effect A (Internet access at home: yes vs. no)

The main effect means were very close for those with Internet versus for those without Internet: 47.88 versus 47.74. These means were not significantly different, $F(1, 560) = 0.008$, $p = 0.931$. The null hypothesis for main effect A failed to reject; therefore the effect of Internet access was not a determinant factor for student NCE test performance. Details are in Appendix F—Primary Factorial ANOVA.

Main Effect B (Income of household: three categories)

The main effect means for the three income categories $0–$20,000, $20,001–$30,000, and $30,001+ were 46.36, 47.56, and 49.52, respectively. These means were not significantly different, $F(2, 560) = 1.729, p = 0.178$. The null hypothesis for main effect B failed to reject; therefore the effect of household income was not a determinant factor for student NCE test performance. Post hoc comparisons were not discussed due to the non-significant result, however, such comparisons were performed. Details are in Appendix F—Primary Factorial ANOVA.

Main Effect C (Highest level of education attained: two categories)

The main effect means for the two education categories were 44.60 for those with a 2-year post secondary degree or less, and 51.02 for those with a bachelor's degree or greater. These means were significantly different, $F(1, 560) = 18.250, p < 0.001$. The null Hypothesis for the main effect C was rejected; therefore the effect of education level of parent/guardian was a factor related to student NCE test performance. Further details are in Appendix F—Primary Factorial ANOVA.

Interaction Effects

The following results for each interaction effect include the means, and levels of significance. Post hoc comparisons were presented if the results were proven to be significant.

AB Interaction (Internet and Income)

The AB Interaction means ranged from a low of 45.15 for those with Internet and the lowest income to a high of 50.63 for those with Internet and the highest income. These means were not significantly different, $F(2, 560) = 0.901$, $p = 0.407$. The null hypothesis for the interaction effect failed to reject; therefore the interaction effect of Internet access and household income was not a determinant factor for student NCE test performance. Graphing the means indicated potential interactions; details are available in Appendix G—Primary Interaction Graphs for Factors A & B. Post hoc comparisons were not discussed due to the non-significant result, however such comparisons were performed. Details are in Appendix F—Primary Factorial ANOVA.

AC Interaction (Internet and Education)

The AC Interaction means ranged from a low of 43.26 for those without Internet and the lowest education level to a high of 51.54 for those without Internet and the highest education level. These means were not significantly different, $F(1, 560) = 0.614$, $p = 0.434$. The null hypothesis for the interaction effect failed to reject; therefore the interaction effect of Internet access and the highest attained level education in the household was not a determinant factor for student NCE test performance. Graphing the means indicated a potential interaction; details are available in Appendix H—Primary Interaction Graphs for Factors A & C. Analysis details are in Appendix F—Primary Factorial ANOVA.

BC Interaction (Income and Education)

The BC Interaction means ranged from a low of 42.10 for those with the lowest income and lowest education level to a high of 52.79 for those with the highest income and the highest education level. These means were not significantly different, $F(2, 560) = 0.612$, $p = 0.542$. The null hypothesis for the interaction effect failed to reject; therefore the interaction effect of household income and the highest attained level education in the household was not a determinant factor for student NCE test performance. Graphing the means indicated a potential interaction, however, the results were not significant; details are available in Appendix I—Primary Interaction Graphs for Factors B & C. Post hoc comparisons were not discussed due to the non-significant result, however such comparisons were performed. Further details are in Appendix F—Primary Factorial ANOVA.

ABC Interaction (Internet, Income, and Education)

The ABC Interaction means ranged from a low of 40.78 for those without Internet, lowest income and lowest education level to a high of 55.67 for those with Internet, the highest income and the highest education level. These means were significantly different, $F(2, 560) = 3.234$, $p = 0.040$. The null hypothesis for the interaction effect was rejected; therefore the interaction effect of Internet access, household income, and the highest attained level education in the household was a factor related to student NCE test performance. Graphing the means indicated the potential of interactions, and post hoc comparisons evidenced three interactions. Details are available in Appendix J—Primary Interaction Graphs for Factors A & B & C.

Scheffé's post hoc comparison was too conservative to be of use because the critical difference was larger than most groups; for example, 53.87. The Scheffé's post hoc critical difference was so large due to the large n (572), and the disparate differences among group sizes (ranging from 19 to 124). The critical difference for Tukey's post hoc comparison was 12.02. Tukey's test yielded results that indicated three differences among the 12 means: (1) those without Internet, lowest income, and lowest education were different from those without Internet, lowest income, and highest education, (2) those without Internet, lowest income, and lowest education were different from those with Internet, highest income, and highest education, and (3) those with Internet, lowest income, and lowest education were different from those with Internet, highest income, and highest education. Details are available in Appendix K—Tukey's Post Hoc Comparison on Primary ABC Interaction.

Measures of Association

The Partial η^2 score estimates the portion of the variance due to the factors in the analysis. The Partial η^2 scores were all very small. The largest was 0.032 for the main effect on Education—saying that 3.2% of the variability can be attributed to education differences. The other significant finding, the ABC interaction, was 0.011. All other Partial η^2 scores were >0.006. By this estimation, only 5.5% of the variability is explained by the factors of the analysis. Further details are in Appendix F—Primary Factorial ANOVA.

Summary of Primary Factorial ANOVA

There were two significant differences in students NCE total scores: (1) the main effect for the education level of the parent and/or guardian, $F(1, 544) = 20.412, p < 0.001$ and (2) the three-way interaction of the factors of Internet access at home, household income and highest level of parent education, $F(2, 560) = 3.234, p = 0.040$. The education level of the parent and / or guardian proved to far exceed the level of rejection in this study. It is also worth noting that only 5.5% of the variability is explained by the factors of the analysis.

One-Way ANOVAs on Uncategorized and Categorized Data

The data were collapsed in to coarse categories to meet the requirement of being fully crossed. Revealing results were found in performing one-way ANOVAs on all three factors in the raw categorical form. Further, the factorial ANOVA results are based upon the means of each cell, and the n of the cells were different, one-way ANOVAs performed on each of the factors will yield different results than that of the main effects in the factorial ANOVA. Two sets of one-way ANOVAs are presented to address these issues: (1) Three one-way ANOVAs on the uncategorized full set data for all three factors and (2) Two one-way ANOVAs on categorized full set data of the factors of income and education.

One-Way ANOVA on Uncategorized Full Set Data

The data were grouped according to the requirements of the factorial ANOVA method in the previous analysis. The groupings were three income categories, and two education categories. However, there were seven categories of household income, and six categories of highest level of education in the raw data. Internet access had only two categories: Yes and No. The raw data income categories were: (1) $0–10,000, (2) $10,000–20,000, (3) $20,000–30,000, (4) $30,000–40,000, (5) $40,000–50,000, (6) $50,000–60,000, and (7) Above $60,000. The raw data highest level of education categories were: (1) Finished Elementary School, (2) Graduated From High School, (3) Attended College or training after High School, (4) Completed a 2-year college or training program, (5) Completed a 4-year degree at a college or University, and (6) Attended or completed a College Graduate Program.

The next sections present three one-way ANOVAs on Internet, Income, and Education with the full dataset, and all the categories of each factor. Post hoc test were performed to determine which categories were different.

One-Way ANOVA of Uncategorized Internet Access on Full Data Set

The one-way ANOVA for Internet access at home contained 296 without Internet and 276 with Internet. The means were 45.25 and 49.36, respectively. These means were significantly different, $F(1, 570) = 9.535, p = 0.002$. Levene's test of equality of error variances produced a significance result of $F(1, 570 = 6.836), p = 0.009$. This was less than alpha 0.05, therefore the assumption of homogeneity is invalid and results should be treated with extreme caution. Full results of this analysis are available in Appendix L— One-Way ANOVA on Uncategorized Full Set Data.

One-Way ANOVA of Uncategorized Income on Full Data Set

The one-way ANOVA for household income contained seven categories: (1) $0–$10,000, (2) $10,000–$20,000, (3) $20,000–$30,000, (4) $30,000–$40,000, (5) $40,000–$50,000, (6) $50,000–$60,000, and (7) Above $60,000. The n and mean of these categories were: (1) $n = 88, \mu = 40.83$, (2) $n = 122$, $\mu = 45.50$, (3) $n = 132, \mu = 46.67$, (4) $n = 54, \mu = 51.28$, (5) $n = 74$, $\mu = 43.70$, (6) $n = 34, \mu = 51.03$, and (7) $n = 68, \mu = 58.43$. These means were significantly different, $F(6, 565) = 10.589, p < 0.001$. Levene's test of equality of error variances produced a significance result of $F(6, 565 = 2.318), p = 0.032$. This was less than alpha 0.05, therefore the assumption of homogeneity is invalid and results should be treated with caution. Full results of this analysis are available in Appendix L—One-way ANOVA on Uncategorized Full Set Data.

Post hoc comparisons were performed to determine which of the income means were different; there were seven categories of income. The results of Scheffé's method indicate that the lowest third and the fifth income categories were different, $p < 0.001$, from the highest category ($60,000+). Full results of this analysis are available in Appendix L—One-way ANOVA on Uncategorized Full Set Data.

One-Way ANOVA of Uncategorized Education Access on Full Data Set

The one-way ANOVA for education of parent/guardian, contained six categories: (1) Finished Elementary School, (2) Graduated From High School, (3) Attended College or training after High School, (4) Completed a 2-year college or training program, (5) Completed a 4-year degree at a college or University, and (6) Attended or completed a College Graduate Program. The n and mean of these categories were: (1) $n = 12$, $\mu = 46.00$, (2) $n = 99$, $\mu = 41.48$, (3) $n = 120$, $\mu = 42.21$, (4) $n = 102$, $\mu = 46.90$, (5) $n = 100$, $\mu = 50.66$, and (6) $n = 139$, $\mu = 53.54$. These means were significantly different, $F(5, 566) = 11.035$, $p < 0.001$. Levene's test of equality of error variances produced a significance result of $F(5, 566 = 0.707)$, $p = 0.618$. This was more than alpha 0.05, therefore the assumption of homogeneity is valid. Full results of this analysis are available in Appendix L—One-way ANOVA on Uncategorized Full Set Data.

Post hoc comparisons were performed to determine which of the parent / guardian education means were different; there were six categories of education. The results of Scheffé's method indicate that the second and third education category was different from the top two categories five and six, $p = 0.004$ and $p < 0.001$, $p = 0.006$, and $p < 0.001$, respectively. Full results of this analysis are available in Appendix L—One-way ANOVA on Uncategorized Full Set Data. Therefore, the parent/guardian education categories were differences centered about the bachelors' level of education. The exception was the lowest group, which had a relatively small n.

One-Way ANOVA on Categorized Full Set Data

The factorial ANOVA results are based upon the means of each cell. Because the n of the cells were different, one-way ANOVAs performed on the factors of income and education will yield different results than that of the main effects in the factorial ANOVA. Because the factor of Internet access was not collapsed (data was yes vs. no) it would yield the same result as the previous section and is not presented here.

One-Way ANOVA of Categorized Income on Full Data Set

The one-way ANOVA for household income contained 210 in the lowest income category, 132 in the middle-income category, and 230 in the highest income category. The means were 43.54, 46.67, and 50.93, respectively. These means were significantly different, $F(2, 569) = 12.178$, $p < 0.001$. Levene's test of equality of error variances produced a significance result of $F(2, 569 = 6.663)$, $p = 0.001$. This was less than alpha 0.05, therefore the assumption of homogeneity is invalid and results should be treated with caution. Full results of this analysis are available in Appendix M—One-way ANOVA on categorized full set data.

Post hoc comparisons were performed to determine which of the income means were different; there were three categories of income. The results of Scheffé's method indicate that the lowest income and middle-income categories were not different, $p = 0.201$. The comparisons of the lowest income category and the highest income category were different, $p < 0.001$. Comparisons of the middle-income income category and the highest income category were also different, $p = 0.048$. Full results of this analysis are available in Appendix M—One-way ANOVA on categorized full set data. Therefore, low-income category and the middle-income category were not significantly different. However, the low-income category and the high-income category were significantly different, and the middle-income category and the high-income category were significantly different.

One-Way ANOVA of Categorized Education Access on Full Data Set

The one-way ANOVA for the factor C, Education of Parent / Guardian, contained 333 in the category with a 2-year degree or less and 239 in the category with a bachelor's or greater. The means were 43.57 and 52.33, respectively. These means were significantly different, $F(1, 570) = 44.812$, $p < 0.001$. Levene's test of equality of error variances produced a significance result of $F(1, 570 = 0.789)$, $p = 0.375$. This was greater than alpha 0.05, therefore the assumption of homogeneity is valid. Full results of this analysis are available in Appendix M—One-way ANOVA on categorized full set data.

Summary of One-way ANOVAs on Uncategorized and Categorized Data

The results from all these analyses were very significant; $p < 0.001$. However, Internet and income, both uncategorized and categorized, broke the assumption of homogeneity. These findings support the literature presented in Chapter Two.

RESULTS OF FURTHER ANALYSIS WITH OUTLIERS REMOVED

Two troubling features existed in the data from the primary analysis: an excess number of outlying data points, and the assumption of homosce-dasticity could be challenged by other methods. The following sections and analyses present findings that are a result of trimming questionable data. Other analyses presented address issues with the design of the factorial model; namely, the design being unbalanced.

Assumption of Homoscedasticity Part 2

An additional test to prove that groups have equal variance is Hartley's Test for Homogeneity of Variance as specified by Wearden (1991, pp. 350–351) and Winer (1971, pp. 206–208) to prove homoscedasticity. The null hypothesis for Hartley's Test is that the variances of the groups are equal as illustrated in Equation 1.

$$H_0 : \sigma_1^2 = \sigma_2^2 = \sigma_3^2 = \sigma_n^2 \tag{1}$$

The critical F_{max} Statistics illustrated in Equation 2 shows the range of rejection. Commonly published tables (Wearden, 1991, p. 591, Winer, 1971, p. 875) contain distribution tables for the F_{max} Statistic in a range up to 12 groups and 60 observations. The average number of observations in the cells of the distribution was 46.3. Tables display a critical statistic for 30 and then 60 degrees of freedom. Given that the number of degrees of freedom for this distribution fall between the available critical statistics, both are displayed. If the distribution meets the more rigorous number, then homoscedasticity is proven.

$$F_{max_{.01.12.60}} = 2.7 \text{ to } F_{max_{.01.12.30}} = 4.2 \tag{2}$$

The average degrees of freedom were greater than 30. Equation 3 details results that indicate that the critical statistic for 30 degrees of freedom was not met. Therefore, the second assumption for ANOVA, homoscedasticity, was not met.

$$F_{max} = \frac{\text{Largest Variance}}{\text{Smallest Variance}} = \frac{371.49}{78.48} = 4.73 < F_{max_{.01.12.30}} = 4.2 \tag{3}$$

To meet the homoscedasticity requirement, data from both ends were removed, such that the distribution would be of equal variance. A quick glance at the histogram indicates an abundance of data on the extremes. Precisely, 9 values of "1" and 3 values of "99" were removed. Additionally, these values did not seem to be valid—perhaps these students did not understand the directions to the test, or purposefully answered incorrectly. For these reasons, homoscedasticity and validity, these data were removed or trimmed from both ends as specified by Winer (1971, p. 51). The calculated result of Equation 4 indicated that the critical value might have been in the proper range. The value is valid for 30 degrees of freedom, but not 60 degrees of freedom. Because the average degrees of freedom were near 45, the value may or may not have met the requirement.

$$F_{max} = \frac{\text{Largest Variance}}{\text{Smallest Variance}} = \frac{291.15}{73.61} = 3.95 < F_{max_{.01,12,30}} = 4.2 \qquad (4)$$

Levene's test of equality of error variances was performed on the first data trim set, which had the 9 values of 1, and 3 values of 99 removed. Levene's test of homogeneity of variance produced a significance result of $p = 0.026$. This was less than the required 0.05, therefore the assumption of homogeneity was invalid ($F_{11, 548} = 2.009$). Full results of this analysis are available in Appendix N—Analysis: First Trimmed Dataset.

Because the homoscedasticity requirement was still not yet met, the data were trimmed again to ±3 standard deviations of the mean. This resulted in removing two scores of "3", and two scores of "92" The second factorial ANOVA produced an acceptable result of Levene's test of equality of error variances, $p = 0.052$. That result was greater than alpha 0.05; therefore the assumption of homogeneity is valid ($F_{11, 544} = 1.794$). Full results of this analysis are available in Appendix O—Unbalanced Factorial ANOVA. With the improved trim homoscedasticity is met. The results from this improved set (second trim) were used for analysis of data. As for the concerns of normality, with this data set, 100% of the distribution is ±3 standard deviations. Figure 8 illustrates the new distribution.

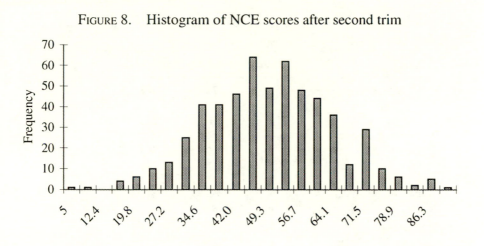

FIGURE 8.   Histogram of NCE scores after second trim

Data for Further Analyses

The distribution was arranged according to the dashed rectangles that group cells in Tables 6 and 7. The results of the data trimming process are shown in Table 10, Distribution of Data for Main Effects Second Trim. The data removed was nearly even (9 and 7) for Effect A. Effect A had a distribution of 267 for those with Internet versus 289 for those without Internet access. The data removed for Effect B was 4 in the first category, 1 in the second category, and 11 in the third category. Effect B has a distribution of 206 for those in the lowest income, 131 for those in the second category, and 219 for the third category. The data removed for Effect C was 12 in the first category, and 4 in the second category. Effect C has a distribution of 321 for those with lowest education level and 235 for those with highest education level.

Table 11, Distribution of Data—Count in each cell illustrates, the *n* of each cell to be used in the analysis of data. Originally, each cell was targeted to have at least 20 observations. This was nearly achieved; only one cell contained less than 20. Those without Internet, in the $20,001–$30,000 income category and with a bachelor's degree or greater comprise a group of 19. Four other groups were near the requirement of 20 that contained between 23 and 25 observations. Two groups had a much larger number of observations. Those without Internet, $0–$20,000 income and a 2-year degree or

TABLE 10. Distribution of Data for Main Effects Second Trim

Effect	Category	Full Set	Second Trim	Change
Effect A—Internet Access at Home	1	276	267	9
Effect A—No Internet Access at Home	0	296	289	7
Effect B—$0–$20,000	1	210	206	4
Effect B—$20,001–$30,000	2	132	131	1
Effect B—$30,001+	3	230	219	11
Effect C—2-Year Degree or Less	1	333	321	12
Effect C—Bachelor's Degree or Greater	2	239	235	4

less comprise a group of 121. Also worth noting is the group with Internet, $30,001 + income, and bachelor's or greater whom comprise a group of 94. Comparison of cells such as those with / without Internet and low income and low education reveals a difference of 84 (37 vs. 121). Because the factorial ANOVA compares the means of the cells, the effect of different numbers of observations with cells will only affect the degrees of freedom.

Unbalanced Main Effects

The results of each of the three main effects are briefly presented. Results presented on each main effect are: means, levels of significance, and post hoc comparisons if the results proved to be significant.

Unbalanced Main Effect A (Internet access at home: yes vs. no)

The main effect means were very close for those with Internet versus for those without Internet: 48.37 versus 47.69. These means were not significantly different, $F(1, 544) = 0.261$, $p = 0.610$. The null hypothesis for the main effect A failed to reject; therefore the effect of Internet access was not a determinant factor for student NCE test performance. Details are in Appendix O—Unbalanced Factorial ANOVA.

TABLE 11.   Distribution of Data—Count in Each Cell

	Internet Access			No Internet Access		
	$0–$20K	$20–$30K	$30K+	$0–$20K	$20–$30K	$30K+
Elementary School— High School, Some College—2-Year Degree	37	38	51	121	50	24
4-Year Degree—Graduate Program	23	24	94	25	19	50

Unbalanced Main Effect B (Income of household: three categories)

The main effect means for the three income categories $0–$20,000, $20,001–$30,000, and $30,001+ were 46.89, 47.78, and 49.41, respectively. These means were not significantly different, $F(2, 544) = 1.389, p = 0.248$. The null hypothesis for the main effect B failed to reject; therefore the effect of household income was not a determinant factor for student NCE test performance. Post hoc comparisons were not discussed due to the non-significant result, however such comparisons were performed. Details are in Appendix O—Unbalanced Factorial ANOVA.

Unbalanced Main Effect C (Highest level of education attained: two categories)

The main effect means for the two education categories were 45.02 for those with a 2-year post secondary degree or less, and 51.03 for those with a bachelor's degree or greater. These means were significantly different, $F(1, 544) = 20.412, p < 0.001$. The null hypothesis for the main effect C was rejected; therefore the effect of education level of parent / guardian was a factor related to student NCE test performance. Further details are in Appendix O—Unbalanced Factorial ANOVA.

Unbalanced Interaction Effects

The following results for each interaction effect include the means, and levels of significance. Post hoc comparisons were presented if the results were proven to be significant.

Unbalanced AB Interaction (Internet and Income)

The AB Interaction means ranged from a low of 45.72 for those with Internet and the lowest income to a high of 51.52 for those with Internet and the highest income. These means were not significantly different, $F(2, 544) = 2.337$, $p = 0.098$. The null hypothesis for the interaction effect failed to reject; therefore the interaction effect of Internet access and household income was not a determinant factor for student NCE test performance. Graphing the means indicated potential interactions; details are available in Appendix P—Unbalanced Interaction Graphs for Factors A & B. Post hoc comparisons were not discussed due to the non-significant result, however such comparisons were performed. Details are in Appendix O—Unbalanced Factorial ANOVA.

Unbalanced AC Interaction (Internet and Education)

The AC Interaction means ranged from a low of 43.85 for those without Internet and the lowest education level to a high of 51.53 for those without Internet and the highest education level. These means were not significantly different, $F(1, 544) = 1.591$, $p = 0.208$. The null hypothesis for the interaction effect failed to reject; therefore the interaction effect of Internet access and the highest attained level education in the household was not a determinant factor for student NCE test performance. Graphing the means indicated a potential interaction; details are available in Appendix Q—Unbalanced Interaction Graphs for Factors A & C. Analysis details are in Appendix O—Unbalanced Factorial ANOVA.

Unbalanced BC Interaction (Income and Education)

The BC Interaction means ranged from a low of 43.17 for those with the lowest income and lowest education level to a high of 52.81 for those with the highest income and the highest education level. These means were not significantly different, $F(2, 544) = 0.651$, $p = 0.522$. The null hypothesis for the interaction effect failed to reject; therefore the interaction effect of household income and the highest attained level education in the household was not a determinant factor for student NCE test performance. Graphing the means indicated a potential interactions, however, the results were not significant; details are available in Appendix R—Unbalanced Interaction Graphs for Factors B & C. Post hoc comparisons were not discussed due to the non-significant result, however such comparisons were performed. Further details are in Appendix O—Unbalanced Factorial ANOVA.

Unbalanced ABC Interaction (Internet, Income, and Education)

The ABC Interaction means ranged from a low of 41.77 for those without Internet, lowest income and lowest education level to a high of 55.67 for those with Internet, the highest income and the highest education level. These means were not significantly different, $F(2, 544) = 2.453, p = 0.087$. The null hypothesis for the interaction effect failed to reject; therefore the interaction effect of Internet access, household income, and the highest attained level education in the household was not a determinant factor for student NCE test performance. Graphing the means indicated the potential of interactions, however, the results were not significant. Details are available in Appendix S—Unbalanced Interaction Graphs for Factors A,B & C. Post hoc comparisons were not discussed due to the non-significant 1, however such comparisons were performed. Further details are in Appendix O—Unbalanced Factorial ANOVA.

Unbalanced Measures of Association

The Partial η^2 scores were all very small. The largest was 0.036 for the main effect on Education—saying that 3.6% of the variability can be attributed to education differences. Both the Internet–income interaction and the Internet–income–education interaction have a Partial η^2 value of 0.009—almost 1% of the variability can be attributed to each of these interactions. By this estimation, only 6.4% of the variability is explained by the factors of the analysis. Further details are in Appendix O—Unbalanced Factorial ANOVA.

Summary of Unbalance Factorial ANOVA

The only significant difference in students' NCE total score was the main effect for the education level of the parent and / or guardian. It proved to far exceed the level of rejection in this study, $F(1, 544) = 20.412, p < 0.001$.

The other result that proved close was the three-way interaction of all independent variables, $F(2, 544) = 2.453$, $p = 0.087$. Although the result was not significant, it is of interest because it indicates a weak link to support the notion that an interaction of all the factors contributes to student NCE test performance.

OTHER ANALYSIS

The unbalanced factorial ANOVA compares the means of the cells, and it will yield a different main effect result than a one-way ANOVA performed upon the same data. Essentially factorial ANOVA does not perform a weighting for of the distribution of groups. Because of this difference, results from one-way ANOVA on the data of main effects are presented.

An additional ABC factorial ANOVA was conducted. In this factorial ANOVA the cells were balanced. Hays (1988, p. 430) and Winer (1971, p. 314) expressed an extreme preference for a factorial ANOVA design that is both fully crossed and balanced. Thus, the results of a fully crossed and balanced factorial ANOVA can be contrasted with the crossed-unbalanced factorial ANOVA. Table 12, Differences in n of cells shows the difference in the number of observations between the unbalanced and the fully crossed and balanced factorial ANOVA. The extreme differences are exemplified in the cell for those without Internet access and the lowest income and education, containing 102 more data points than the extreme least populated cell.

Finally, another set of one-way ANOVAs was performed with the data used from the fully crossed and balanced factorial ANOVA. The differences

TABLE 12.   Differences in *n* of Cells

	Internet Access			No Internet Access		
	$0–$20K	$20–$30K	$30K+	$0–$20K	$20–$30K	$30K+
Elementary School–High School, Some College–2-Year Degree	18	19	32	102	31	5
4-Year Degree–Graduate Program	4	5	75	6	-	31

of *n* in certain categories could have "pulled" the results to favor a category with a greater *n* than other categories, and the lack equality of variance was also a concern with the results of the first set of one-way ANOVAs. The results of these one-way ANOVA analyses of the fully crossed and balanced data set were compared to the results of the both fully crossed-unbalanced and fully crossed-balanced factorial ANOVA.

One-Way ANOVA on Main Effects

One-Way ANOVA analyses were conducted on each of the factors with the same data used to calculate the main effects in the Factorial ANOVA. Specifically, the second trimmed set that met the requirements for ANOVA. Each one-way ANOVA produced results significant beyond 0.001. Details of this analysis are in Appendix T—One-Way ANOVA for Factors A, B, & C.

One-Way ANOVA for Internet Access

The one-way ANOVA for the factor A, Internet access at home, contained 289 without Internet and 267 with Internet. The means were 45.63 and 49.93, respectively. These means were significantly different, $F(1, 544) = 13.057, p < 0.001$. Levene's test of equality of error variances produced a significance result of $F(1, 554 = 7.389), p = 0.007$. This was less than alpha 0.05, therefore the assumption of homogeneity is invalid and results should be treated with extreme caution. Full results of this analysis are available in Appendix T—One-Way ANOVA for Factors A, B, & C.

One-Way ANOVA for Income

The one-way ANOVA for the factor B, household income, contained 206 in the lowest income category, 131 in the middle-income category, and 219 in the highest income category. The means were 44.37, 47.02, and 51.23, respectively. These means were significantly different, $F(2, 554) = 13.208, p < 0.001$. Levene's test of equality of error variances produced a significance result of $F(2, 553 = 3.375), p = 0.035$. This was less than alpha 0.05, therefore the assumption of homogeneity is invalid and results should be treated with caution. Full results of this analysis are available in Appendix T—One-Way ANOVA for Factors A, B, & C.

Post hoc comparisons were performed to determine which of the income means were different; there were three categories of income. The post hoc comparison will determine which categories are significantly different. Scheffé's method for comparing means was selected because it is regarded as conservative method (Hays, 1988, pp. 415–418, Wearden, 1991, pp. 308–309). Scheffé's method for comparing means uses a null hypothesis stating two other means combined and divided by two equal the mean being examined for difference. Stated mathematically in illustrated in Equation 5:

$$H_0 : \mu_1 - \frac{\mu_2}{2} - \frac{\mu_3}{2} = 0 \tag{5}$$

The results of Scheffé's method indicate that the lowest income and middle-income categories were not different, $p = 0.232$. The comparisons of the lowest income category and the highest income category were different, $p < 0.001$. Comparisons of the middle-income category and the highest income category were also different, $p = 0.023$. Full results of this analysis are available in Appendix T—One-Way ANOVA for Factors A, B, & C. Therefore, low-income category and the middle-income category were not significantly different. However, the low-income category and the high-income category were significantly different, and the middle-income category and the high-income category were significantly different.

One-Way ANOVA for Education of Parent / Guardian

The one-way ANOVA for the factor C, Education of Parent / Guardian, contained 321 in the category with a 2-year degree or less and 235 in the category with a bachelor's or greater. The means were 44.29 and 52.36, respectively. These means were significantly different, $F(1, 254) = 47.733$, $p < 0.001$. Levene's test of equality of error variances produced a significance result of $F(1, 554 = 3.983)$, $p = 0.046$. This was less than alpha 0.05, therefore the assumption of homogeneity is invalid however, it is within the range of rounding error. Full results of this analysis are available in Appendix T—One-Way ANOVA for Factors A, B, & C.

Summary of One-way ANOVA

The results from all three analyses were significant, though two broke the assumption of homogeneity. Levene's test of equality of error variances was very close for education, $p = 0.046$ within rounding error for the expected 0.050. Income was also close, $p = 0.035$, however Internet was not close, $p = 0.007$. These results support the results of the unbalance factorial ANOVA.

Results of the Fully Crossed and Balanced Factorial AVOVA

To balance a factorial ANOVA each cell must have an equal n; contain the same number of data sets. In this case, the n of each cell as set to the smallest complete data set of 19; the group without Internet, income of $20,001–$30,000, and an education level of bachelor's or greater. The other cells were populated with pseudo-random selections from their complete datasets containing similar means and variances. The selection was based upon the mean and standard deviation being within a range of 1.00 of the original values for the entire dataset.

For this fully crossed and balanced distribution, Levene's test of equality of error variances produced a result of $F(11, 216 = 1.248)$, $p = 0.257$. This was greater than alpha 0.05, therefore the assumption of homogeneity is valid. Full results of this analysis are available in Appendix U—Fully Crossed and Balanced A & B & C Factorial ANOVA.

Main Effects of the Fully Crossed and Balanced Factorial AVOVA

The results of each of the three main effects of the fully crossed and balanced factorial AVOVA are briefly presented. Results on each main effect included the means, levels of significance and post hoc comparisons if the results proved to be significant.

Fully Crossed and Balanced Main Effect A (Internet)

The main effect means were very close for those without Internet versus for those with Internet: 47.79 versus 48.83. These means were not significantly different, $F(1, 216) = 0.331$, $p = 0.566$. The null hypothesis for the main effect A failed to reject; therefore the effect of Internet access was not a determinant factor for student NCE test performance. Details are in Appendix U—Fully Crossed and Balanced A & B & C Factorial ANOVA.

Fully Crossed and Balanced Main Effect B (Income)

The main effect means for the three income categories $0–$20,000, $20,001–$30,000, and $30,001+ were 46.79, 48.03, and 50.11, respectively. These means were not significantly different, $F(2, 216) = 1.155$, $p = 0.317$. The null hypothesis for the main effect B failed to reject; therefore the effect of household income was not a determinant factor for student NCE test performance. Post hoc comparisons were not discussed due to the non-significant result, however such comparisons were performed. Details are in Appendix U—Fully Crossed and Balanced A & B & C Factorial ANOVA.

Fully Crossed and Balanced Main Effect C (Education)

The main effect means for the two education categories were 45.49 for those with a 2-year post secondary degree or less, and 51.12 for those with a bachelor's degree or greater. These means were significantly different, $F(1, 216) = 9.787$, $p = 0.002$. The null hypothesis for the main effect C was rejected; therefore the effect of education level of parent / guardian was a factor related to student NCE test performance. Further details are in Appendix U—Fully Crossed and Balanced A & B & C Factorial ANOVA.

Interaction Effects of the Fully Crossed and Balanced Factorial AVOVA

The results of each of the fully crossed and balanced factorial AVOVA interaction effects will be briefly presented. Results on each interaction effect included the means, levels of significance and post hoc comparisons if the results proved to be significant.

Fully Crossed and Balanced AB Interaction (Internet and Income)

The AB Interaction means ranged from a low of 45.95 for those with Internet and the lowest income to a high of 52.32 for those with Internet and the highest income. These means were not significantly different, $F(2, 216) = 0.993$, $p = 0.372$. The null hypothesis for the interaction effect AB failed to reject; therefore the interaction effect of Internet access and household income was not a determinant factor for student NCE test performance. Post hoc comparisons were not discussed due to the non-significant result, however such comparisons were performed. Details are in Appendix U— Fully Crossed and Balanced A & B & C Factorial ANOVA.

Fully Crossed and Balanced AC Interaction (Internet and Education)

The AC Interaction means ranged from a low of 44.04 for those without Internet and the lowest education level to a high of 51.54 for those without Internet and the highest education level. These means were not significantly different, $F(1, 216) = 1.087$, $p = 0.298$. The null hypothesis for the interaction effect AC failed to reject; therefore the interaction effect of Internet access and the highest attained level education in the household was not a determinant factor for student NCE test performance. Further details are in Appendix U—Fully Crossed and Balanced A & B & C Factorial ANOVA.

Fully Crossed and Balanced BC Interaction (Income and Education)

The BC Interaction means ranged from a low of 43.21 for those with lowest income and lowest education level to a high of 53.29 for those with the highest income and the highest education level. These means were not significantly different, $F(2, 216) = 0.411$, $p = 0.663$. The null hypothesis for the interaction effect BC failed to reject; therefore the interaction effect of household income and the highest attained level education in the house-hold was not a determinant factor for student NCE test performance. Post hoc comparisons were not discussed due to the non-significant result, however such comparisons were performed. Further details are in Appendix U—Fully Crossed and Balanced A & B & C Factorial ANOVA.

Fully Crossed and Balanced ABC Interaction (Internet, Income, and Education)

The ABC Interaction means were ranged from a low of 40.84 for those without Internet, lowest income and lowest education level to a high of 56.74 for those with Internet, the highest income and the highest education level. These means were not significantly different, $F(2, 216) = 2.037$, $p = 0.133$. The null hypothesis for the interaction effect failed to reject;

therefore the interaction effect of Internet access, household income, and the highest attained level education in the household was not a determinant factor for student NCE test performance. Post hoc comparisons were not discussed due to the non-significant result, however such comparisons were performed. Further details are in Appendix U—Fully Crossed and Balanced A & B & C Factorial ANOVA.

Fully Crossed and Balanced Measures of Association

The Partial η^2 scores were all very small. The largest was 0.043 for the main effect on education, indicating that 4.3% of the variability can be attributed to education differences. Internet–income–education interaction had a Partial η^2 value of 0.019—almost 2% of the variability can be attributed to this interaction. Internet–income interaction had a Partial η^2 value of 0.011—about 1% of the variability can be attributed to this interaction. By this estimation, only 9.3% of the variability was explained by the factors of the analysis. Conversely, 90% of the variability in the NCE total score is apparently due to factors not considered in this research. Further details are in Appendix U—Fully Crossed and Balanced A & B & C Factorial ANOVA.

Summary of the Fully Crossed and Balanced Factorial AVOVA

Although the dataset was severely trimmed the results were essentially the same as the first unbalanced factorial ANOVA. Levene's test of equality of error variances produced a far better result, $F(1, 216) = 1.248$, $p = 0.257$, which was much greater than the required 0.05. The only independent variable which had a significant effect on the dependent variable was education, $F(1, 216) = 9.787$, $p = 0.002$. This value far exceeded the established alpha of 0.05. No other result was close to the required alpha. While these results were essentially the same findings as the unbalanced factorial ANOVA, however in this analysis the homoscedasticity assumption was clearly met.

One-Way ANOVA Results with Fully Crossed and Balanced Data

Because two of the three of the first three one-way ANOVA analyses did not meet the requirement of homoscedasticity, it is prudent to calculate results based upon the fully crossed and balanced data set. This dataset possessed means and variances similar to the original set, and contained only 19 samples per cell. In the prior analysis, Fully Crossed and Balanced Factorial AVOVA, the findings were similar to the unbalanced factorial ANOVA, however the homoscedasticity assumption was improved. The prior one-way ANOVA produced lower p values, however the homoscedasticity requirement was broken for two of the factors. The next three sections present the results of those analyses.

One-way ANOVA for Internet Access with Fully Crossed
and Balanced Data

The one-way ANOVA for the factor A, Internet access at home, contained 114 without Internet and 114 with Internet. The means were 47.79 and 48.82, respectively. These means were not significantly different, $F(1, 226) = 0.317$, $p = 0.574$. Levene's test of equality of error variances produced a significance result of $F(1, 226 = 1.684)$, $p = 0.196$. This was greater than 0.05, therefore the assumption of homogeneity is valid. Full results of this analysis are available in Appendix V—One-Way ANOVA—Balanced Data.

One-way ANOVA for Income with Fully Crossed and Balanced Data

The one-way ANOVA for the factor B, household income, contained 76 in the lowest income category, 76 in the middle-income category, and 76 in the highest income category. The means were 46.79, 48.03, and 50.11, respectively. These means were not significantly different, $F(2, 225) = 1.110$, $p = 0.311$. Levene's test of equality of error variances produced a significance result of $F(2, 225 = 2.097)$, $p = 0.125$. This was greater than 0.05, therefore the assumption of homogeneity is valid. A post hoc comparison was not performed because the result was not significant. Full results of this analysis are available in Appendix V—One-Way ANOVA—Balanced Data.

One-way ANOVA for Education of Parent / Guardian with Fully Crossed and Balanced Data

The one-way ANOVA for the factor C, Education of Parent / Guardian, contained 114 in the category with a 2-year degree or less and 114 in the category with a bachelor's or greater. The means were 45.49 and 51.12, respectively. These means were significantly different, $F(1, 226) = 9.760$, $p = 0.002$. Levene's test of equality of error variances produced a significance result of $F(1, 226 = 0.005)$, $p = 0.942$. This was greater than 0.05, therefore the assumption of homogeneity is valid. Full results of this analysis are available in Appendix V—One-Way ANOVA—Balanced Data.

Summary of One-Way ANOVA Results with Fully Crossed and Balanced Data

Education of Parent / Guardian proved to be a significant factor [$F(1, 226) = 9.760$, $p = 0.002$] in the analysis of the data, even when the data had been severely trimmed. The assumption of homogeneity was valid; $p = 0.942$. While the other two factors, Internet access and household income were not significant; the assumption of homogeneity was valid for both.

SUMMARY OF ANALYSES

Many analyses were presented in this chapter. Table 13, Summary of Analyses is provided to briefly summarize these findings. Results that were valid and significant are indicated with an X. The cells indicated with "*" did calculate significant results, however, they did not meet the assumption of homoscedasticity (groups have equal variance); therefore those results

TABLE 13.   Summary of Analyses

	Factors						
	A	B	C	AB	AC	BC	ABC
Primary Factorial ANOVA			X				X
Uncategorized One-Way ANOVA	*	*	X				
Categorized One-Way ANOVA		*	X				
Unbalanced Factorial ANOVA			X				
One-way ANOVA on Unbalanced Factorial Data	*	*	X				
Fully Crossed and Balanced Factorial ANOVA			X				
One-way ANOVA on Fully Crossed and Balanced Data			X				

should be treated cautiously. It is worth noting that the One-way ANOVA on Unbalanced Factorial data for education was rounded up to meet the assumption of Homoscedasticity; the calculated value was $p = 0.047$ and needed to meet or exceed 0.050.

The significant ABC interaction, $F(2, 560) = 3.234, p = 0.040$, in the primary analysis included outliers. After the outliers were removed, the other two three-way interactions were not significant; $p = 0.087$ in the unbalanced factorial ANOVA, and $p = 0.113$ in the fully crossed and balanced factorial ANOVA. The outliers were perhaps the result of students did not understand the directions to the test, or purposefully answered incorrectly.

The general trend revealed in Table 13 from the analyses of data was that Factor C, highest attained education in household, was significant in all analyses. Students from homes where the parent / guardian had completed at least a bachelors degree scored significantly higher NCE total test scores than students from homes where the highest level of education was less than a bachelors degree.

For this study Factor A was Internet access at home, Factor B was household income, and Factor C was highest education attained within the household. AB was the results of the combined interaction of A and B, AC was the results of the combined interaction of A and C, BC was the results of the combined interaction of B and C, and ABC was the results of the combined interaction of A, B and C.

FINDINGS RELATED TO HYPOTHESES AND RESEARCH QUESTION

The research question of this study was: What are the differences among the standardized test scores of students due to factors of Internet access at home, household income, and the highest level of education attained by mother, father, or guardian? Results were mostly consistent among all the various analysis performed. The significant difference in student standardized test performance was the attained education level of their parent / guardian. This finding was consistent in all five analyses presented.

The other significant difference was the three-way interaction of Internet access at home, household income, and the highest level of education in the student home. However, other analyses performed after outlying data were removed did not reveal significant differences. Because this result was apparently the result of the outliers, the validity was suspect.

The primary analysis accounted for only 5.5% of the observed variability. In the best-case scenario, the fully crossed and balanced analysis, 90% of the effects observed were attributed to something other than the factors of this study. This begs the question *what accounts for all this other variance?*

Contrast of Findings from Analyses

Table 14, Detailed Summary of Findings, Main Effects and One-Way ANOVAs, Table 15, Detailed Summary of Findings, Interactions in Primary Factorial ANOVAs, and Table 16, Detailed Summary of Findings, Interactions in Unbalanced and Fully Crossed and Balanced Factorial ANOVAs show for each factor and combination of factors in all the analyses: (1) mean, (2) n, (3) Levene's test of homogeneity of variance, and (4) the significance.

As the various challenges to validity (outliers and unbalanced factorial ANOVA) were addressed in the various analyses, one finding clearly distilled out: the level of the parents' education was the significant factor in determining a students NCE test performance.

The Factorial ANOVA compared the means of each cell within the matrix, whereas the one-way ANOVA does not weight the factors in accordance to categories set in the factorial analyses. An instance of this effect of the different methods is shown in Table 12, by comparing the means for Internet access at home. In the unbalanced factorial ANOVA, the means for Internet access at home were calculated as a mean of the cells (yes vs. no), and the one-way ANOVA on unbalanced factorial data calculates the mean based on all the individual data points. The means for the unbalanced factorial ANOVA were $\mu_{yes} = 48.37$, $\mu_{no} = 47.69$, and for the one-way ANOVA $\mu_{yes} = 49.93$, $\mu_{no} = 45.63$. The differences between these means were 0.68 for the factorial ANOVA versus 4.3 for the one-way ANOVA.

OTHER FINDINGS

The analyses conducted beyond those originally planned for this study were revealing. Although the balanced factorial ANOVA analyses yielded

TABLE 14. Detailed Summary of Findings, Main Effects
and One-Way ANOVAs

Factors		
A (Internet)	**B (Income)**	**C (Education)**

Primary Factorial ANOVA Main Effects

$\mu_{yes} = 47.88$, $\mu_{no} = 47.75$	$\mu_1 = 46.36$, $\mu_2 = 47.56$, $\mu_3 = 49.52$	$\mu_1 = 44.60$, $\mu_2 = 51.02$
$n_{yes} = 296$, $n_{no} = 276$	$n_1 = 210$, $n_2 = 132$, $n_3 = 230$	$n_1 = 333$, $n_2 = 239$
$L = 0.063$	$L = 0.063$	$L = 0.063$
$p = 0.931$	$p = 0.178$	$p < 0.001$

Unbalanced Factorial ANOVA Main Effects

$\mu_{yes} = 48.37$, $\mu_{no} = 47.69$	$\mu_1 = 46.89$, $\mu_2 = 47.78$, $\mu_3 = 49.41$	$\mu_1 = 45.02$, $\mu_2 = 51.03$
$n_{yes} = 289$, $n_{no} = 267$	$n_1 = 206$, $n_2 = 131$, $n_3 = 219$	$n_1 = 321$, $n_2 = 235$
$L = 0.052$	$L = 0.052$	$L = 0.052$
$p = 0.610$	$p = 0.248$	$p < 0.001$

One-Way ANOVA on Unbalanced Factorial Data

$\mu_{yes} = 49.93$, $\mu_{no} = 45.63$	$\mu_1 = 44.37$, $\mu_2 = 47.02$, $\mu_3 = 51.23$	$\mu_1 = 44.29$, $\mu_2 = 52.36$
$n_{yes} = 267$, $n_{no} = 289$	$n_1 = 206$, $n_2 = 131$, $n_3 = 219$	$n_1 = 321$, $n_2 = 235$
$L = 0.007$	$L = 0.035$	$L = 0.046$
$p < 0.001$	$p < 0.001$	$p < 0.001$

Fully Crossed and Balanced Factorial ANOVA Main Effects

$\mu_{yes} = 47.79$, $\mu_{no} = 48.82$	$\mu_1 = 46.79$, $\mu_2 = 48.03$, $\mu_3 = 50.10$	$\mu_1 = 45.49$, $\mu_2 = 51.12$
$n_{yes} = 114$, $n_{no} = 114$	$n_1 = 76$, $n_2 = 76$, $n_3 = 76$	$n_1 = 114$, $n_2 = 114$
$L = 0.257$	$L = 0.257$	$L = 0.257$
$p = 0.566$	$p = 0.317$	$p = 0.002$

One-Way ANOVA on Fully Crossed and Balanced Data

$\mu_{yes} = 48.82$, $\mu_{no} = 47.79$	$\mu_1 = 46.79$, $\mu_2 = 48.03$, $\mu_3 = 50.11$	$\mu_1 = 45.49$, $\mu_2 = 51.12$
$n_{yes} = 114$, $n_{no} = 114$	$n_1 = 76$, $n_2 = 76$, $n_3 = 76$	$n_1 = 114$, $n_2 = 114$
$L = 0.196$	$L = 0.125$	$L = 0.942$
$p = 0.574$	$p = 0.125$	$p = 0.002$

Note: μ is the mean, n is the number of datasets per analysis, L is the results Levene's test of homogeneity of variance (0.050 or better is required), and p is the significance result (0.050 of less is required).

TABLE 15.   Detailed Summary of Findings, Interactions in Primary Factorial ANOVAs

AB (Internet and Income)	AC (Internet and Education)	BC (Income and Education)	ABC (Internet, Income, and Education)
Primary Factorial ANOVA			
$\mu_{AyB1} = 45.15$,	$\mu_{AyC1} = 45.26$,	$\mu_{B1C1} = 42.10$,	$\mu_{AyB1C1} = 43.42$, $\mu_{AyB1C2} = 46.87$,
$\mu_{AyB2} = 47.86$,	$\mu_{AyC2} = 50.53$,	$\mu_{B1C2} = 50.62$,	$\mu_{AyB2C1} = 46.76$, $\mu_{AyB2C2} = 48.96$,
$\mu_{AyB3} = 50.68$,	$\mu_{AnC1} = 43.95$,	$\mu_{B2C1} = 45.46$,	$\mu_{AyB3C1} = 45.60$, $\mu_{AyB3C2} = 55.77$,
$\mu_{AnB1} = 47.57$,	$\mu_{AnC2} = 51.54$	$\mu_{B2C2} = 49.66$,	$\mu_{AnB1C1} = 40.78$, $\mu_{AnB1C2} = 54.36$,
$\mu_{AnB2} = 47.27$,		$\mu_{B3C1} = 46.26$,	$\mu_{AnB2C1} = 44.16$, $\mu_{AnB2C2} = 50.37$,
$\mu_{AyB3} = 48.41$		$\mu_{B3C2} = 52.83$	$\mu_{AnB3C1} = 46.92$, $\mu_{AnB3C2} = 49.90$
$n_{AyB1} = 61$,	$n_{AyC1} = 133$,	$n_{B1C1} = 162$,	$n_{AyB1C1} = 38$, $n_{AyB1C2} = 23$,
$n_{AyB2} = 62$,	$n_{AyC2} = 143$,	$n_{B1C2} = 48$,	$n_{AyB2C1} = 38$, $n_{AyB2C2} = 24$,
$n_{AyB3} = 153$,	$n_{AnC1} = 200$,	$n_{B2C1} = 89$	$n_{AyB3C1} = 57$, $n_{AyB3C2} = 96$,
$n_{AnB1} = 149$,	$n_{AnC2} = 96$	$n_{B2C2} = 43$,	$n_{AnB1C1} = 124$, $n_{AnB1C2} = 25$,
$n_{AnB2} = 70$,		$n_{B3C1} = 82$,	$n_{AnB2C1} = 51$, $n_{AnB2C2} = 19$,
$n_{AnB3} = 77$		$n_{B3C2} = 148$	$n_{AnB3C1} = 25$, $n_{AnB3C2} = 52$
$L = 0.063$	$L = 0.063$	$L = 0.063$	$L = 0.063$
$p = 0.931$	$p = 0.614$	$p = 0.612$	$p = 0.040$

Note: μ is the mean, n is the number of datasets per analysis, L is the results Levene's test of homogeneity of variance (0.050 or better is required), and p is the significance result (0.050 of less is required).

essentially the same result, it seems to have only lost power for having a smaller n. The balanced factorial ANOVA reinforced the results of the unbalanced. The results of the one-way ANOVA analyses raise interesting issues, especially because they were all significant and only parent / guardian education was significantly different in the factorial analyses.

Discussion of the One-Way ANOVA Findings

The results of one-way ANOVA on the unbalanced data were all significant, but when all is taken into account, two (Internet and income) of the three one-way ANOVAs performed on the unbalanced data set were invalid due to unequal variance. The difference in the method of the factorial ANOVA yields a better comparison of the real nature of the data. That was because the factorial ANOVA compared the cell means and it accounted for differences in the group sizes. For instance, the n for the one-way ANOVA

TABLE 16. Detailed Summary of Findings, Interactions in Unbalanced and Fully Crossed and Balanced Factorial ANOVAs

AB (Internet and Income)	AC (Internet and Education)	BC (Income and Education)	ABC (Internet, Income, and Education)
Unbalanced Factorial ANOVA			
$\mu_{AyB1} = 48.06,$	$\mu_{AyC1} = 51.53,$	$\mu_{B1C1} = 43.17,$	$\mu_{AyB1C1} = 44.57, \mu_{AyB1C2} = 46.87,$
$\mu_{AyB2} = 47.69,$	$\mu_{AyC2} = 50.53,$	$\mu_{B1C2} = 45.89,$	$\mu_{AyB2C1} = 46.76, \mu_{AyB2C2} = 48.96,$
$\mu_{AyB3} = 47.03,$	$\mu_{AnC1} = 43.85,$	$\mu_{B2C1} = 50.61,$	$\mu_{AyB3C1} = 47.27, \mu_{AyB3C2} = 55.77,$
$\mu_{AnB1} = 45.72,$	$\mu_{AnC2} = 46.20$	$\mu_{B2C2} = 49.66,$	$\mu_{AnB1C1} = 41.77, \mu_{AnB1C2} = 54.36,$
$\mu_{AnB2} = 47.86,$		$\mu_{B3C1} = 46.01,$	$\mu_{AnB2C1} = 45.02, \mu_{AnB2C2} = 50.37,$
$\mu_{AyB3} = 51.52$		$\mu_{B3C2} = 52.81$	$\mu_{AnB3C1} = 44.75, \mu_{AnB3C2} = 49.86$
$n_{AyB1} = 60,$	$n_{AyC1} = 126,$	$n_{B1C1} = 158,$	$n_{AyB1C1} = 38, n_{AyB1C2} = 23,$
$n_{AyB2} = 62,$	$n_{AyC2} = 141,$	$n_{B1C2} = 48,$	$n_{AyB2C1} = 38, n_{AyB2C2} = 24,$
$n_{AyB3} = 148,$	$n_{AnC1} = 195,$	$n_{B2C1} = 88$	$n_{AyB3C1} = 51, n_{AyB3C2} = 94,$
$n_{AnB1} = 146,$	$n_{AnC2} = 94$	$n_{B2C2} = 43,$	$n_{AnB1C1} = 121, n_{AnB1C2} = 25,$
$n_{AnB2} = 69$		$n_{B3C1} = 75,$	$n_{AnB2C1} = 50, n_{AnB2C2} = 19,$
$n_{AnB3} = 75$		$n_{B3C2} = 144$	$n_{AnB3C1} = 24, n_{AnB3C2} = 50$
$L = 0.052$	$L = 0.052$	$L = 0.052$	$L = 0.052$
$p = 0.098$	$p = 0.208$	$p = 0.522$	$p = 0.087$
Fully Crossed and Balanced Factorial ANOVA			
$\mu_{AyB1} = 45.95,$	$\mu_{AyC1} = 46.95,$	$\mu_{B1C1} = 43.21,$	$\mu_{AyB1C1} = 45.58, \mu_{AyB1C2} = 46.32,$
$\mu_{AyB2} = 48.21,$	$\mu_{AyC2} = 50.70,$	$\mu_{B1C2} = 50.37,$	$\mu_{AyB2C1} = 47.37, \mu_{AyB2C2} = 49.05,$
$\mu_{AyB3} = 52.31,$	$\mu_{AnC1} = 44.03,$	$\mu_{B2C1} = 46.34,$	$\mu_{AyB3C1} = 47.89, \mu_{AyB3C2} = 56.74,$
$\mu_{AnB1} = 47.84,$	$\mu_{AnC2} = 51.54$	$\mu_{B2C2} = 49.71,$	$\mu_{AnB1C1} = 40.84, \mu_{AnB1C2} = 54.42,$
$\mu_{AnB2} = 47.84,$		$\mu_{B3C1} = 46.92,$	$\mu_{AnB2C1} = 45.32, \mu_{AnB2C2} = 50.37,$
$\mu_{AyB3} = 47.89$		$\mu_{B3C2} = 53.29$	$\mu_{AnB3C1} = 45.95, \mu_{AnB3C2} = 49.84$
$n_{AyB1} = 38,$	$n_{AyC1} = 57,$	$n_{B1C1} = 38,$	$n_{AyB1C1} = 19, n_{AyB1C2} = 19,$
$n_{AyB2} = 38,$	$n_{AyC2} = 57,$	$n_{B1C2} = 38,$	$n_{AyB2C1} = 19, n_{AyB2C2} = 19,$
$n_{AyB3} = 38,$	$n_{AnC1} = 57,$	$n_{B2C1} = 38,$	$n_{AyB3C1} = 19, n_{AyB3C2} = 19,$
$n_{AnB1} = 38,$	$n_{AnC2} = 57$	$n_{B2C2} = 38,$	$n_{AnB1C1} = 19, n_{AnB1C2} = 19,$
$n_{AnB2} = 38,$		$n_{B3C1} = 38,$	$n_{AnB2C1} = 19, n_{AnB2C2} = 19,$
$n_{AnB3} = 38$		$n_{B3C2} = 38$	$n_{AnB3C1} = 19, n_{AnB3C2} = 19$
$L = 0.257$	$L = 0.257$	$L = 0.257$	$L = 0.257$
$p = 0.372$	$p = 0.298$	$p = 0.663$	$p = 0.133$

reports n_{yes} = 267, n_{no} = 289 and this appears to be equal. However, the factorial ANOVA used the mean of the means of the cells, and the n for the cells ranged from n_{AnB2C2} = 19 to the other extreme of n_{AnB1C1} = 124. The method of the factorial ANOVA caused the mean of the cell with an n of 19 to have the same bearing on the outcome as the cell with an n of 124. Essentially the factorial method caused an equal effect for each group, and showed a more comprehensive view of the data in regards to the research question.

The three one-way ANOVAs conducted on the fully crossed and balanced data yielded a similar result; two of the three were not significant. The main differences from fully crossed and balanced one-way ANOVA being: (1) the weighting effect different cell sizes were not a factor and (2) that the data did meet the assumption of homoscedasticity. However, just like the factorial results, only the highest attained education of the parent / guardian was significant.

Other Findings Issues

The GEARUP Program has demonstrated it has a measured effect on the NCE scores of the participants. All student data sets were complete, and therefore received the same treatment. It is assumed that this effect was equally distributed among the participants.

CHAPTER FIVE

CONCLUSIONS, IMPLICATIONS, AND RECOMMENDATIONS

This chapter presents the conclusions, implications, and recommendations of this study. The conclusions are those directly related to the hypothesis and other conclusions derived from the findings. The implications are insights based upon the data as they relate to the larger world. Recommendations are a combination of the implications and conclusions—rational directions to proceed with the results of this research.

REVIEW OF CHAPTERS ONE TO FOUR

The purpose of this study was to examine the differences among the standardized test scores of students due to factors of Internet access at home, household income, and the highest level of education attained by mother, father, or guardian. Nearly every student has Internet access at school, and over half of the nation has an Internet connection at home. If students with Internet access at home have a different academic standing, is it influenced by the Internet connection or family affluence? There are established bodies of evidence that link academic standing with factors of family affluence, that is, parental education and household income.

The population consisted of the participants of the San Miguel GEARUP program at New Mexico Highlands University, located in northern New Mexico. The independent variables were: (A) Internet access grouped as yes versus no, (B) highest level of education within the household grouped as those with or without a bachelor's degree, and (C) household income in three categories ($0–$20,000, $20,001–$30,000, and $30,001+) of annual income. The dependent variable was the NCE total score from Spring 2004 CTB / McGraw-Hill–TerraNova.

There were two significant differences in students NCE total scores: (1) the main effect for the education level of the parent and / or guardian, $F(1,544) = 20.412$, $p < 0.001$ and (2) the three-way interaction of the factors of Internet access at home, household income, and highest level of parent education, $F(2,560) = 3.234$, $p = 0.040$. Only the education level of the parent and / or guardian proved to far exceed the level of rejection in this study. The three-way interaction was suspected because further analyses performed after removing obvious outliers produced no other significant findings. It is also worth noting that only 5.5% of the variability is explained by the factors of the analysis.

Additional analyses were based upon removing outliers which appeared to be of suspect validity; that is, 9 values of "1" on the NCE scale. The other analyses performed were another unbalanced factorial ANOVA, a fully crossed and balanced factorial ANOVA and two sets of one-way ANOVAs. The fully crossed and balanced factorial ANOVA required removing a great deal of data. Findings were consistent among all the various analyses performed. The highest level of education within the household was the only determinant factor of student NCE total score performance in the unbalanced factorial ANOVA, $F(1,544) = 20.412$, $p < 0.001$. The dataset was reduced to create a fully crossed and balance factorial ANOVA. In this analysis the education of the parent / guardian was significant, $F(1,216) = 9.787$, $p = 0.002$. One-way ANOVAs were performed on both sets of data, the unbalanced data set and the fully crossed and balanced data set. Both sets yielded a significant result only for the education of the parent / guardian, $F(1,254) = 47.733$, $p < 0.001$ and $F(1,226) = 9.760$, $p = 0.002$, respectively.

CONCLUSIONS RELATED TO HYPOTHESIS AND RESEARCH QUESTIONS

The null hypothesis states that the means of all groups (main effects and interactions) would be equal. Expressed mathematically:

$$\mu_{0A} = \mu_{0B} = \mu_{0C} = \mu_{0AB} = \mu_{0AC} = \mu_{0BC} = \mu_{0ABC}$$

There were seven parts to the null hypothesis. The two general portions were main effects and interactions: (1) three main effects (A, B, & C), and (2) four interaction effects (AB, AC, BC, & ABC). The three main effects were: (A) Internet access at home, (B) household income, and (C) highest level of education within the household. The interaction effects were: AB—Internet and income, AC—Internet and education, BC—income and education, and ABC—Internet, income, and education. Of the seven parts of the null hypothesis, the one significant finding was main effect C, highest level of education within the household.

The Research Question was: What are the differences among the standardized test scores of students due to factors of Internet access at home, household income, and the highest level of education attained by mother, father, or guardian? The one significant difference was main effect C, highest level of education within the household.

Highest Level of Education Within the Household

There were six levels of education within the raw data. However, to arrange the data for the design, a completely crossed (enough data in every cell) factorial ANOVA, the six levels were collapsed into two categories. The categorical break was coarse; the categories of education for the parent / guardian were either with or without a bachelor's degree.

Highest level of education within the household proved to be of signifi-cance in every form of analysis performed. In the primary analysis, the main effect for the education level of the parent and / or guardian was significant, $F(1,544) = 20.412$, $p < 0.001$. In the unbalanced factorial ANOVA, with the outliers removed, the finding was significant, $F(1,544) = 20.412$, $p < 0.001$.

With a severely reduced dataset in a fully crossed and balanced factorial ANOVA the result was also significant, $F(1,216) = 9.787$, $p = 0.002$. Two one-way ANOVAs were also performed, one on each of the two sets of data (unbalanced and fully crossed and balanced). Both were significant for education of the parent / guardian, $F(1,254) = 47.733$, $p < 0.001$, and $F(1,226) = 9.760$, $p = 0.002$, respectively. These findings support more than 30 years worth of data presented in the Literature Review. Therefore, based upon the data, the education of the parent / guardian will have a far greater impact upon a student's likely test performance than Internet access in the home.

Interaction of Internet, Income, and Education

The three-way interaction of the factors of Internet access at home, household income, and highest level of parent education were significant, $F(2,560) = 3.234$, $p = 0.040$. However, this result is suspect because after removing obvious outliers the result was no longer significant, $p = 0.087$. When the design became fully crossed and balanced, the result was further from significant, $p = 0.113$. Had the result emerged in the other analyses it would not be suspect. There may be an interaction due to the combination of these factors—supporting the notion of a digital divide. However, the parent / guardians education, based upon the data, is a far greater factor.

OTHER CONCLUSIONS

In addition to the hypothesis and research question, there are additional conclusions that can be drawn from the data. These other conclusions relate to the population of the study, cell sizes in the factorial ANOVA, distribution of groups, education stratification, and unaccounted variability.

Population

It is likely that the population of this study is not representative of the general population. If there had been more data in the extreme categories, the design of the factorial ANOVA could have contained more categories. The effect of more categories may have yielded more effects not observed in this study. With enough data to breakout more categories, particular groupings may have proven significant.

Cell Sizes

The extreme differences are exemplified in the cell for those without Internet access and the lowest income and education, containing 102 more data points than the extreme least-populated cell. The fully crossed and balanced factorial controlled for this and yielded similar results. The fully crossed and balanced design with random assignment produced the results that accounted for the most variability.

Distribution of Groups

The collapsing of categories may have been too extreme to detect differences. In the realm of economic groups, three categories may represent a low-, middle-, and high-income category. However, within the population studied, the category definitions do not appear to match the national profile. It would be difficult to argue that $30,000 annual income is the threshold for a high income. The grouping of education category was separated on those with or without a bachelor's degree. Potential effects were not observed because of the collapsed of the data.

Education Stratification

Although the highest attained education within the household proved to be a factor of significance, the groupings were coarse. Other results may surface with more data because the categories of education could be expanded. Such results could reveal more precisely what level of education makes a difference. The raw data contained six different levels of education: (1) finished elementary school, (2) graduated from high school, (3) attended college or training after high school, (4) completed a 2-year college or training program, (5) completed a 4-year degree at a college or university, and (6) attended or completed a college graduate program. With enough data to create more categories, the precise levels of education that differ could be identified. The categories were too coarse to observe potential effects due to various levels of parent / guardian education.

Unaccounted Variability

The Partial η^2 scores were all very small. The largest was 0.032 for the main effect on Education—saying that 3.2% of the variability can be attributed to education differences. The other significant finding, the ABC interaction, was 0.011. All other Partial η^2 scores were above 0.006. By this estimation, only 5.5% of the variability is explained by the factors of the analysis. Conversely, more than 94% of the variability was due to factors not included in this study.

Removing outliers improved the estimation to 6.4% in the unbalance factorial ANOVA. In the fully crossed and balanced ANOVA the estimate was that 9.3% of the variability is explained by the factors of the analysis. The trend of improvement supports better validity in the trimmed data.

IMPLICATIONS

There are five implications presented: (1) highest education within the household matters, (2) confounding factors reveal better results, (3) population size, (4) unaccounted variability, and (5) gifting Internet access would be imprudent. A sub-section of the last implication titled *The Killer App* is an explanation of a concept introduced within that implication.

Highest Education Within the Household Matters

The clear conclusion of this research is that the highest education within the household was the significant finding. The findings on the interactions of Internet access at home and parent / guardian education were far from significant in all analyses. Likewise, the findings on the interaction of income and education were not significant. The three-way interaction of all factors was significant in the primary analysis, but it was not significant in any other analyses. This indicates that parent / guardian education truly stands as the one significant factor in the study.

Confounding Factors Reveal Better Results

The arguments presented by Schield (1999) regarding spurious association appear to be a valid explanation of the results of this study. If factors are viewed in singularity and assumptions are ignored, each factor appears to be significant. In a vacuum, each factor is significant. However, in a more comprehensive analysis, only one factor proves to be determinant.

Although the three-way interaction of Internet, income, and education produced a significant result in one of the five analyses, it is suspect.

The base question of this study was to investigate the contribution of Internet access to a students academic standing. However, it was the confounding factor of parent / guardian education that proved to be significant.

Larger Population Would Improve Quality

If the size of the study was increased, perhaps the "tails" would prove to be significant. Filling the cells in the extremes proved to be difficult, for example, there was a lack of data for (1) low income and higher education levels of the parents and (2) high income and low education. There was also an abundance of data in the category of those without Internet but with low income and low education. In order to conduct an analysis that would contain many categories there would need to be enough data to fill the unlikely extremes. This would also overfill the expected categories and likely require a random assignment process to create the preferred fully crossed and balanced factorial ANOVA.

There are two implications: (1) the population would need to be much larger and (2) a random selection process would be required to balance the data. As a rough estimate from the distribution observed in this study, it may require 20 to 30 times as much data to fill the extremes and provide for the random selection process. Because the data gathered will likely be representative of the general population, there would need to be a random selection process to arrange the data into a fully crossed and balanced ANOVA.

Unaccounted Variability

The accounted variability increased with the data trim and the fully crossed and balanced design. Perhaps a larger population in a fully crossed and balanced design could lead to further improvement. The introduction of other factors, or more categories may also improve the results.

Gifting Internet Access Would Be Imprudent

The San Miguel GEARUP program has considered gifting Internet access to parents / guardians who currently do not have Internet access.

The distribution of this population reveals large portions that were low income and without Internet access; 146 of the 267 without Internet reported an annual household income of less than $20,000. It was believed such households would not likely obtain Internet access for economic reasons. The distribution of Internet access to that population would probably not improve academic standing of the students. However, an effort to raise the education level of their parents may raise the academic standing of their children.

Unless some other factor(s) was / were associated with the act of providing Internet access, there appear to be no solid grounds to expect improvement in student performance. However, if other associated activities or different technologies were present, there may be grounds to expect a difference in student performance. If a new education *killer app* for monitoring student performance and facilitating parent involvement were to accompany the gift, it may be reasonable to expect a difference in student performance. It is also possible that providing education to the parents in concert with a gift of Internet access could facilitate a difference in student performance.

The Killer App

In the development of the personal computer revolution, there have been foundational technical developments often referred to as a "killer app." Spreadsheets (Excel and Lotus 123) are thought to be the killer apps that brought PCs into the business world. Word processors (WordPerfect and MS Word) are thought to be the killer apps that brought PCs onto nearly every desktop, replacing the now outdated typewriters. Email editors (Eudora and Outlook) are the killer apps that brought the Internet and networks to prominence, although both had existed for decades. Web browsers (Netscape and MS Internet Explorer) are thought to be the killer apps that brought the World Wide Web (WWW) to prominence, although the Internet had existed for decades.

Perhaps a killer app for education has yet to emerge. If a new education killer app were to be Internet based it would change the horizon for this study. As in the other realms of PC and Internet use, when the killer app was diffused, the rules changed.

RECOMMENDATIONS

Based on the findings, there are three recommendations for future research: (1) confounding factors, (2) replication, and (3) gifting Internet access must be accompanied.

Confounding Factors

In this study, 94% of the variance was not accounted for by the factors analyzed. Consideration of a design that takes other factors of affluence into account may complicate the design, however, it may improve the applicability to other populations and provide better insight.

The recommendation is to grant further consideration of other factors that may have a greater bearing than reckoned. Some confounding factors may be obvious, and if so, they would be included in quality research. If the confounding factors are not obvious, they should be sought out; that is, student health, curriculum, etc.

Replication With a Larger N

It would seem prudent to replicate this study with a broader population. The essential goal is to create more categories and perhaps reveal trends and interactions. Because the distributions will likely be uneven in categories, as they were in this study, a random selection of categorical data into the cells may be necessary. A $2 \times 4 \times 4$ factorial ANOVA was cited in Chapter Three. The dataset used in this study could not support a design with that many categories. More categories should be used in a replication study to reveal trends not evident in the $2 \times 3 \times 2$ factorial ANOVA used in this study.

The recommendation is to perform the factorial analysis on a larger data set to enable the establishment of more categories. With a factorial design containing more categories, interaction effect(s) may become more evident. Also, the categorical definitions could become more representative of a broader audience.

Replication With a Randomly Assigned Fully Crossed and Balanced Design

Replication with a fully crossed and balanced design is based partially improved Partial η^2 scores observed. It is also not likely to gather data in a fashion that would lead to the exact *n* required for each cell. It would be reasonable to expect that the popular data categories would load up with extra data quickly, and need to be randomly chosen to maintain a balanced design. This supports the prior recommendation of a much larger *N*.

The recommendation is to design the study as a quasi-experimental design, which would gather enough data to allow for the random selection of data into a fully crossed and balanced factorial ANOVA.

Gifting Internet Access Must be Accompanied

The natural diffusion of Internet access into the various categories established in this research indicated that no measurable contribution was made by internet access at home to student academic standing. That is to say, if Internet access is gifted with no additional services, training, programs, or other accompaniments, there is no reason to expect students in the homes receiving the gift to perform differently.

The recommendation is that if Internet access is gifted, it must have some accompaniment. This accompaniment may be parent training / education, some sort of new education killer app, or a combination of such. To form a rational argument for gifting Internet access, which would lead to the expectation of a result different from the conclusions of this research, new factors need to be introduced.

APPENDIX A

Student Application

NMHU/San Miguel GEAR-UP
STUDENT APPLICATION
2003-2004 School Year

CIRCLE SCHOOL: MMS   RHS   WLVHS   WLVMS   WLV Valley   FP

Grade	Last Name	First Name	Middle Name

Mailing Address	City	State	Zip	Phone

Date of Birth:	Gender:	Student ID:	Student Email

With which ethnic group do you identify yourself? (Choose only one)
___ African American ___ Asian / Pacific Islander ___ Anglo ___ Hispanic
___ Native American - Tribe _____ ___ Other _____

Please check if the following is true: Do you participate in a Free / Reduced Lunch Program? _____
Do you have a disability? _____

Are you planning on attending a College / University or Tech School after graduation? ___ Yes ___ No
If yes, what school are you planning to attend?

	Name of Institution	State	Intended Major
1st Choice			
2nd Choice			

If No, please state why. _____

Parent/Guardian Information

Name of First Guardian: _____	Name of Second Guardian: _____
Work Place: _____	Work Place: _____
Work Number: _____	Work Number: _____
Would you like for your child to attend a post secondary institute (college or technical school)?	Would you like for your child to attend a post secondary institute (college or technical school)?
Yes ___ No ___	Yes ___ No ___
If No, why not?	If No, why not?
___ student has a lack of interest	___ student has a lack of interest
___ school is too far away	___ school is too far away
___ costs too much	___ costs too much
___ will be starting or taking care of a family	___ will be starting or taking care of a family
___ student wants to work	___ student wants to work
___ additional education is not necessary	___ additional education is not necessary
___ Other (please complete) _____	___ Other (please complete) _____

Do you have a computer at home? Yes ___ No ___   Do you have Internet access? Yes ___ No ___
Range of Family Income: ___ $0-10,000 ___ $10,000-20,000 ___ $20,000-30,000 ___ $30,000-40,000
___ $40,000-50,000 ___ $50,000-60,000 ___ Above $60,000

Family Educational Information

What is the highest level of education that was received by each family member?

	Finished Elementary School	Graduated from High School	Attended College or training after High School	Completed a 2 year college or training program	Completed a 4 year degree at a college or University	Attended or completed a College Graduate Program
Mother or Guardian						
Father or Guardian						
Grandparents						
Older Brother(s) or Sister(s)						
Other Family Members						

Medical Information

Does the participant have any medical or learning conditions that we should know about in order to ensure that the NMHU / San Miguel GEAR-UP experience is the best we can provide? _____

Name of Physician: _____ Phone: _____

Is the participant taking any medication? If yes, explain: _____

Emergency Contact: _____ Phone: _____ Relationship to participant: _____

Consent / Release

Medical Consent   I authorize all medical, surgical, diagnostic and hospital procedures including ambulance transportation that may be performed or prescribed by a treating physician for the youth listed herein if I cannot be reached in an emergency.

Liability Release   I waive all rights and release all claims that might be held against the school district and the NMHU / San Miguel GEAR-UP Project Partnership, its hired or contracted instructors, staff, volunteers, agencies and their employees and agents, for any and all injuries or losses which may be suffered because of my child's participation in the above activity.

Photo/Video Release   I authorize NMHU / San Miguel GEAR-UP to use my child's photo and / or name for promotional reasons.

Trip Release   I give permission for my child to go on scheduled field trips.

School Release   I authorize my child's school district to release information about my child's grades and progress in school to NMHU / San Miguel GEAR-UP for the purpose of evaluating the student's progress. This information will remain confidential and will be used only for program evaluation.

We certify that the above is true to the best of our knowledge, as well as give permission to NMHU / San Miguel GEAR-UP and it's funding agencies to acquire information about the above's academic performance from middle school and testing agencies for the purpose of evaluating programs sponsored by NMHU/San Miguel GEAR-UP.

Student Signature   Date   Parent Signature   Date   Teacher Signature   Date

Source: San Miguel / New Mexico Highlands University GEARUP Partnership, 2004.

APPENDIX B

INTERNET ACCESS QUERY

SELECT   tDemographicQuery.QueryShortDescription, tStudents.
        tDemographicResults.Result
FROM   tDemographicResults INNER JOIN
        tDemographicQuery ON
        tDemographicResults.QueryID = tDemographicQuery.QueryID
          INNER JOIN
        tStudents ON tDemographicResults.surStudentID = tStudents.
          surStudentID INNER JOIN
        tPeople ON tStudents.PersonID = tPeople.PersonID
WHERE   (tDemographicQuery.QueryShortDescription = 'InternetAccess')

APPENDIX C

INCOME QUERY

SELECT   tStudents.surStudentID, tDemographicLookups.LookUpValue

FROM   tDemographicResults INNER JOIN

tDemographicQuery ON tDemographicResults.QueryID = tDemographicQuery.QueryID INNER JOIN

tDemographicLookups ON tDemographicResults.Result = tDemographicLookups.LookUpValueID INNER JOIN

tStudents ON tDemographicResults.surStudentID = tStudents.surStudentID INNER JOIN

tPeople ON tStudents.PersonID = tPeople.PersonID

WHERE   (tDemographicQuery.QueryShortDescription='IncomeRange') AND (tDemographicResults.Result = 'c26899aa-0e2c-4e36-8f28-edc0b329bffa') OR

(tDemographicResults.Result='5c1d6402-08ff-4227-9111-095b74801c8c') OR

(tDemographicResults.Result='7e61806d-9937-4f22-ad55-0ab6479a7131') OR

(tDemographicResults.Result = '85aabf35-9fca-45cd-aa2c-4a3a52be3c2d') OR

(tDemographicResults.Result = '3CC17E06-FCF7-4FBF-866C-50269E204A87') OR

(tDemographicResults.Result='c949c67e-be7d-4f80-9a87-61bcdf78defa') OR

(tDemographicResults.Result = 'fefedb51-ef4a-482a-b341-6ad4d776b1c0')

ORDER BY tStudents.StudentID

APPENDIX D

EDUCATION QUERY

SELECT   tStudents.surStudentID, tDemographicLookups.Description, tDemographicLookups.ListOrder, tDemographicQuery. QueryShortDescription

FROM   tDemographicResults INNER JOIN tDemographicQuery ON tDemographicResults.QueryID = tDemographicQuery.QueryID INNER JOIN tDemographicLookups ON tDemographicResults.Result = tDemographicLookups.LookUpValueID INNER JOIN tStudents ON tDemographicResults.surStudentID = tStudents.surStudentID INNER JOIN tPeople ON tStudents.PersonID = tPeople.PersonID

WHERE   (tDemographicResults.Result = '99057a14-4d0d-4752-81ec-464224414a1e') OR (tDemographicResults.Result='a9721ca3-ad06-4c92-ba26-4e0d07c3267c') OR (tDemographicResults.Result = 'a247ff4c-e2c7-4e2f-adef-5c37c5ab9df6') OR (tDemographicResults.Result = 'd4788e1a-7d99-41b8-8be9-691abc6586de') OR (tDemographicResults.Result = 'be51792e-b240-4520-b716-bc9b761cf0ae') OR (tDemographicResults.Result = '4dbb122d-1630-4672-b92e-e1688215ed92')

ORDER BY   tStudents.StudentID

APPENDIX E

NCE TEST SCORES QUERY

PART 1

SELECT   [2004_GRT_Master_Fixed_ID].[NCE Total Score], Internet.
          [Got-it], income.income, [Parent education].[Edu-descrpt],
          Internet.[Student ID]
FROM   ((Internet INNER JOIN 2004_GRT_Master_Fixed_ID
          ON Internet.[Student ID] = [2004_GRT_Master_
          Fixed_ID].[Student ID]) INNER JOIN income ON
          Internet.[Student ID] = income.[Student ID]) INNER JOIN
          [Parent education] ON income.[Student ID] = [Parent
          education].[Student ID];

PART 2

SELECT   [full distd].Internet, [full distd].income, [full distd].educa-
          tion, Count([full distd].education) AS CountOfeducation
FROM   [full distd]
GROUP BY [full distd].Internet, [full distd].income, [full distd].education
ORDER BY [full distd].Internet, [full distd].income, [full distd].education;

APPENDIX F

PRIMARY FACTORIAL ANOVA

Univariate Analysis of Variance

Between-Subjects Factors

		N
Internet @ home	0	296
	1	276
Income	1	210
	2	132
	3	230
Education	1	333
	2	239

Levene's Test of Equality of Error Variances[a]

Dependent Variable: NCE total

F	df1	df2	Sig.
1.732	11	560	.063

Tests the null hypothesis that the error variance of the dependent variable is equal across groups.

[a] Design: Intercept + Internet @ home + income + education + Internet @ home * income + Internet @ home * education + income * education + Internet @ home * income * education

Descriptive Statistics

Dependent Variable: NCE total

Internet @ home	Income	Education	Mean	Std. Deviation	N
0	1	1	40.78	13.594	124
		2	54.36	14.688	25
		Total	43.06	14.645	149
	2	1	44.16	13.646	51
		2	50.37	8.858	19
		Total	45.84	12.773	70
	3	1	46.92	16.060	25
		2	49.90	16.161	52
		Total	48.94	16.084	77
	Total	1	42.41	14.039	200
		2	51.16	14.604	96
		Total	45.25	14.780	296
1	1	1	43.42	15.848	38
		2	46.87	11.760	23
		Total	44.72	14.437	61
	2	1	46.76	14.325	38
		2	48.96	12.338	24
		Total	47.61	13.529	62
	3	1	45.60	19.274	57
		2	55.67	17.552	96
		Total	51.92	18.795	153
	Total	1	45.31	16.947	133
		2	53.13	16.304	143
		Total	49.36	17.042	276
Total	1	1	41.40	14.148	162
		2	50.77	13.755	48
		Total	43.54	14.570	210
	2	1	45.27	13.920	89
		2	49.58	10.839	43
		Total	46.67	13.113	132
	3	1	46.00	18.266	82
		2	53.64	17.243	148
		Total	50.92	17.953	230
	Total	1	43.57	15.308	333
		2	52.33	15.642	239
		Total	47.23	16.030	572

Tests of Between-Subjects Effects

Dependent Variable: NCE total

Source	Type III Sum of Squares	df	Mean Square	F	Sig.	Partial Eta Squared	Noncent. Parameter	Observed Power[a]
Corrected Model	15088.381[b]	11	1371.671	5.835	.000	.103	64.187	1.000
Intercept	953475.585	1	953475.585	4056.136	.000	.879	4056.136	1.000
Internet @ home	1.780	1	1.780	.008	.931	.000	.008	.051
Income	812.697	2	406.348	1.729	.178	.006	3.457	.363
Education	4290.099	1	4290.099	18.250	.000	.032	18.250	.989
Internet @ home * income	423.610	2	211.805	.901	.407	.003	1.802	.206
Internet @ home * education	144.331	1	144.331	.614	.434	.001	.614	.123
Income * education	287.888	2	143.944	.612	.542	.002	1.225	.152
Internet @ home * income * education	1520.543	2	760.271	3.234	.040	.011	6.468	.616
Error	131639.158	560	235.070					
Total	1422714.000	572						
Corrected Total	146727.538	571						

[a] Computed using alpha = .05.
[b] R Squared = .103 (Adjusted R Squared = .085).

ESTIMATED MARGINAL MEANS

1. Grand Mean

Dependent Variable: NCE total

Mean	Std. Error	95% Confidence Interval	
		Lower Bound	Upper Bound
47.814	.751	46.339	49.289

2. Internet @ home

Dependent Variable: NCE total

Internet @ home	Mean	Std. Error	95% Confidence Interval	
			Lower Bound	Upper Bound
0	47.749	1.083	45.622	49.875
1	47.879	1.040	45.836	49.923

3. Income

Dependent Variable: NCE total

Income	Mean	Std. Error	95% Confidence Interval	
			Lower Bound	Upper Bound
1	46.358	1.316	43.774	48.943
2	47.562	1.435	44.742	50.381
3	49.522	1.132	47.299	51.745

4. Education

Dependent Variable: NCE total

Education	Mean	Std. Error	95% Confidence Interval	
			Lower Bound	Upper Bound
1	44.607	.949	42.743	46.470
2	51.021	1.164	48.735	53.307

5. Internet @ home * Income

Dependent Variable: NCE total

Internet @ home	Income	Mean	Std. Error	95% Confidence Interval	
				Lower Bound	Upper Bound
0	1	47.571	1.681	44.270	50.872
	2	47.263	2.060	43.216	51.310
	3	48.412	1.866	44.747	52.077
1	1	45.145	2.025	41.167	49.123
	2	47.861	1.999	43.935	51.787
	3	50.632	1.282	48.114	53.149

6. Internet @ home * Education

Dependent Variable: NCE total

Internet @ home	Education	Mean	Std. Error	95% Confidence Interval	
				Lower Bound	Upper Bound
0	1	43.953	1.329	41.342	46.564
	2	51.544	1.709	48.187	54.902
1	1	45.260	1.354	42.601	47.919
	2	50.498	1.580	47.395	53.601

7. Income * Education

Dependent Variable: NCE total

Income	Education	Mean	Std. Error	95% Confidence Interval	
				Lower Bound	Upper Bound
1	1	42.102	1.421	39.310	44.894
	2	50.615	2.215	46.264	54.965
2	1	45.460	1.643	42.233	48.687
	2	49.663	2.354	45.039	54.287
3	1	46.258	1.839	42.646	49.870
	2	52.785	1.320	50.193	55.378

8. Internet @ home * Income * Education

Dependent Variable: NCE total

Internet @ home	Income	Education	Mean	Std. Error	95% Confidence Interval	
					Lower Bound	Upper Bound
0	1	1	40.782	1.377	38.078	43.487
		2	54.360	3.066	48.337	60.383
	2	1	44.157	2.147	39.940	48.374
		2	50.368	3.517	43.460	57.277
	3	1	46.920	3.066	40.897	52.943
		2	49.904	2.126	45.728	54.080
1	1	1	43.421	2.487	38.536	48.306
		2	46.870	3.197	40.590	53.149
	2	1	46.763	2.487	41.878	51.648
		2	48.958	3.130	42.811	55.106
	3	1	45.596	2.031	41.608	49.585
		2	55.667	1.565	52.593	58.740

Post Hoc Tests—INCOME

Multiple Comparisons

Dependent Variable: NCE total

	Income (I)	Income (J)	Mean Difference (I–J)	Std. Error	Sig.	95% Confidence Interval Lower Bound	95% Confidence Interval Upper Bound
Tukey HSD	1	2	–3.13	1.703	.158	–7.13	.87
		3	–7.37*	1.463	.000	–10.81	–3.94
	2	1	3.13	1.703	.158	–.87	7.13
		3	–4.24*	1.674	.031	–8.18	–.31
	3	1	7.37*	1.463	.000	3.94	10.81
		2	4.24*	1.674	.031	.31	8.18
Scheffe	1	2	–3.13	1.703	.185	–7.31	1.05
		3	–7.37*	1.463	.000	–10.97	–3.78
	2	1	3.13	1.703	.185	–1.05	7.31
		3	–4.24*	1.674	.041	–8.35	–.13
	3	1	7.37*	1.463	.000	3.78	10.97
		2	4.24*	1.674	.041	.13	8.35

Based on observed means.
* The mean difference is significant at the .05 level.

Homogeneous Subsets

NCE Total

	Income	N	Subset 1	Subset 2
Student-Newman-Keuls[a,b,c]	1	210	43.54	
	2	132	46.67	
	3	230		50.92
	Sig.		.053	1.000
Tukey HSD[a,b,c]	1	210	43.54	
	2	132	46.67	
	3	230		50.92
	Sig.		.129	1.000
Scheffe[a,b,c]	1	210	43.54	
	2	132	46.67	
	3	230		50.92
	Sig.		.154	1.000

Means for groups in homogeneous subsets are displayed.
Based on Type III Sum of Squares
The error term is Mean Square (Error) = 235.070.
[a] Uses Harmonic Mean Sample Size = 179.797.
[b] The group sizes are unequal. The harmonic mean of the group sizes is used. Type I error levels are not guaranteed.
[c] Alpha = .05.

APPENDIX G

PRIMARY INTERACTION GRAPHS
FOR FACTORS A & B

Primary AB Interaction Data: Internet & Income,
on NCE Total Scale

Internet	No	Yes	No	Yes	No	Yes
Income Category	1	1	2	2	3	3
Mean	47.57	45.15	47.27	47.86	48.41	50.68
N	149	61	70	62	77	153

Primary Interaction Chart: Internet & Income, on NCE Total Scale

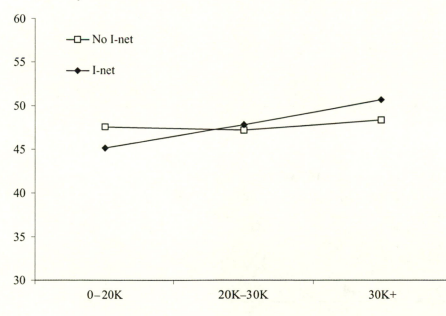

Primary Interaction Chart Data: Internet &
Income, on NCE Total Scale

	0–20K	20–30K	30K+
No I-net	47.57	47.27	48.41
I-net	45.15	47.86	50.68

Primary Interaction Chart: Income & Internet, on NCE Total Scale

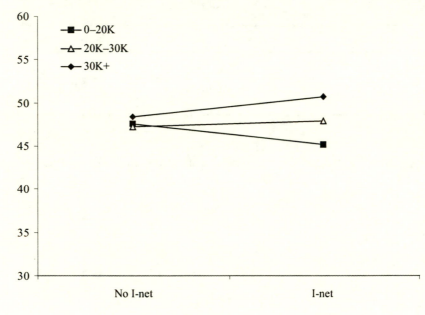

Primary Interaction Chart Data:
Income & Internet, on NCE Total Scale

	No I-net	I-net
0–20K	47.57	45.15
20–30K	47.27	47.86
30k+	48.41	50.68

APPENDIX H

PRIMARY INTERACTION GRAPHS
FOR FACTORS A & C

Primary AC Interaction Data: Internet & Education,
on NCE Total Scale

Internet	No	Yes	No	Yes
Education Category	1	1	2	2
Mean	43.95	45.26	51.54	50.53
N	200	133	96	143

Primary Interaction Chart: Internet & Education, on NCE Total Scale

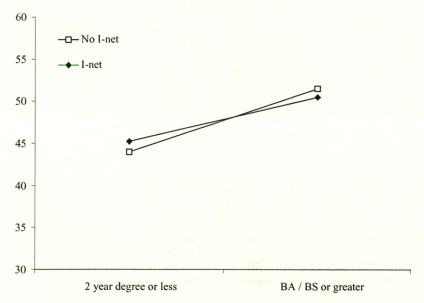

Primary Interaction Chart Data: Internet & Education,
on NCE Total Scale

	2-Year Degree or Less	BA / BS or Greater
No I-net	43.95	51.54
I-net	45.26	50.53

Primary Interaction Chart: Education & Internet, on NCE Total Scale

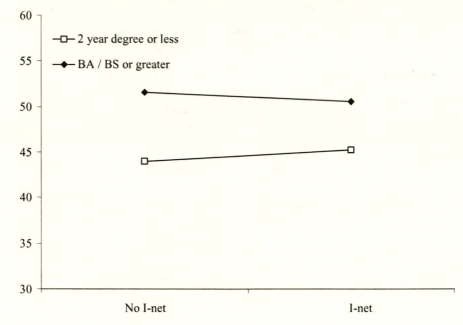

Primary Interaction Chart Data: Education &
Internet, on NCE Total Scale

	No I-net	I-net
2-Year Degree or Less	43.95	45.26
BA / BS or Greater	51.54	50.53

APPENDIX I

PRIMARY INTERACTION GRAPHS
FOR FACTORS B & C

Primary BC Interaction Data: Income & Education,
on NCE Total Scale

Income Category	1	1	2	2	3	3
Education Category	1	2	1	2	1	2
Mean	42.10	50.62	45.46	49.66	46.26	52.83
N	162	48	89	43	82	148

Primary Interaction Chart: Income & Education, on NCE Total Scale

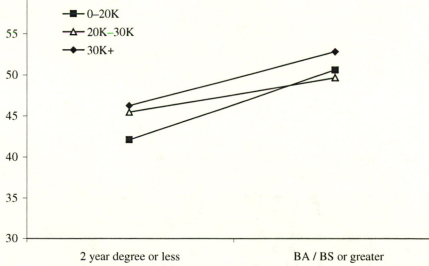

Primary Interaction Chart Data: Income & Education,
on NCE Total Scale

	2 year degree or less	BA / BS or greater
0–20K	42.10	50.62
20–30K	45.46	49.66
30k+	46.26	52.83

Primary Interaction Chart: Education & Income, on NCE Total Scale

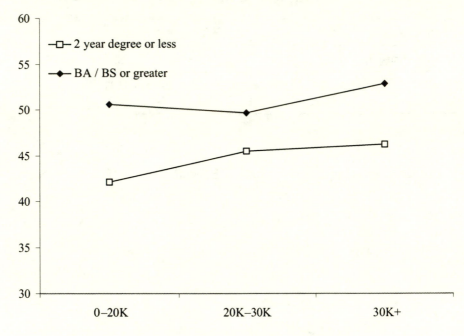

Primary Interaction Chart Data: Education & Income,
on NCE Total Scale

	0–20K	20–30K	30K+
2 year degree or less	42.10	45.46	46.26
BA / BS or greater	50.62	49.66	52.83

APPENDIX J

Primary Interaction Graphs
for Factors A & B & C

Primary ABC Interaction Data: Internet, Income & Education,
on NCE Total Scale

Internet	TRUE			FALSE		
Income	0–20K	20–30K	30K+	0–20K	20–30K	30K+
Elementary School—High School— Some College—2-Year Degree	43.42	46.76	45.60	40.78	44.16	46.92
4-Year Degree— Graduate Program	46.87	48.96	55.77	54.36	50.37	49.90

Primary Interaction Chart: Internet, Income & Education, on NCE Total Scale

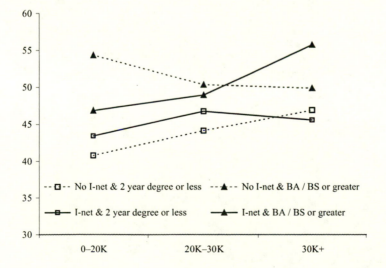

Primary Interaction Chart Data: Internet, Income &
Education, on NCE Total Scale

	0–20K	20–30K	30K+
No I-net & 2 year degree or less	40.78	44.16	46.92
No I-net & BA / BS or greater	54.36	50.37	49.90
I-net & 2 year degree or less	43.42	46.76	45.60
I-net & BA / BS or greater	46.87	48.96	55.77

Primary Interaction Chart: Internet, Income & Education, on NCE Total Scale

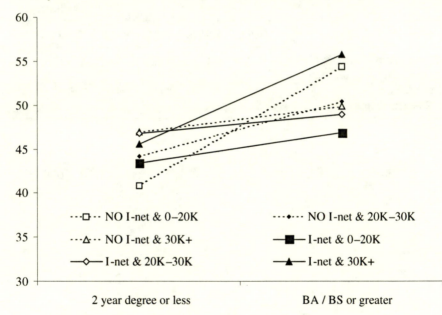

Primary Interaction Chart Data: Internet, Income &
Education, on NCE Total Scale

	2 year degree or less	BA / BS or greater
NO I-net & 0–20K	40.78	54.36
NO I-net & 20–30K	44.16	50.37
NO I-net & 30k+	46.92	49.90
I-net & 0–20K	43.42	46.87
I-net & 20–30K	46.76	48.96
I-net & 30k+	45.60	55.77

Primary Interaction Chart: Internet, Income & Education, on NCE Total Scale

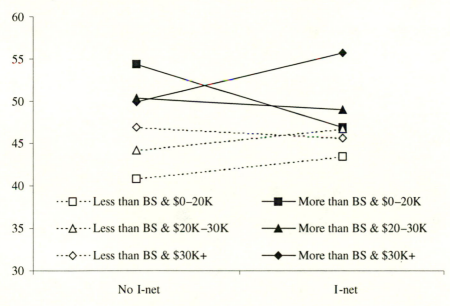

Appendix

Primary Interaction Chart Data: Internet, Income & Education, on NCE Total Scale

	No-Internet at home	Internet at home
Less than BS & $0–20K	40.78	43.42
More than BS & $0–20K	54.36	46.87
Less than BS & $20–30K	44.16	46.76
More than BS & $20–30K	50.37	48.96
Less than BS & $30k+	46.92	45.60
More than BS & $30k+	49.90	55.77

APPENDIX K

TUKEY'S POST HOC COMPARISON
ON PRIMARY ABC INTERACTION

SPSS did not calculate the post on the 3-way interaction. Therefore, the comparison was performed on Microsoft Excel. Critical difference was calculated as follows:

$$\text{Critical difference} = q_r \sqrt{\frac{MS_{\text{within group error}}}{n_{\text{(per group)}}}}$$

where:

q_r Significant Studentized Ranges for Tukey Multiple-Comparison Tests.

$MS_{\text{within group error}}$, taken from the SPSS output.

n, the groups have different n, therefore a harmonic mean was calculated.

q_r was found to be 4.62, where $r = 12$ (number of groups that were compared) and $df = \infty$. While the actual $df = 572$, the table for Significant Studentized Ranges for Tukey Multiple-Comparison Tests (Bruning & Kintz, 1997, p. 344) listed df in the increment from 60, 120, and ∞.

$MS_{\text{within group error}}$ was taken from the SPSS output on the Primary Factorial ANOVA.

The calculation for a harmonic mean was specified (Bruning & Kintz, 1997, p. 195) as follows:

$$\text{harmonic mean} = \bar{n} = \frac{\text{number of groups}}{\dfrac{1}{n_1} + \dfrac{1}{n_2} + \dfrac{1}{n_3} + \dfrac{1}{n_4} + \dfrac{1}{n_5} + \ldots + \dfrac{1}{n_n}}$$

Therefore the harmonic mean for this study would be

$$\overline{n} = \frac{12}{\frac{1}{124} + \frac{1}{25} + \frac{1}{51} + \frac{1}{19} + \frac{1}{25} + \frac{1}{52} + \frac{1}{38} + \frac{1}{23} + \frac{1}{38} + \frac{1}{24} + \frac{1}{57} + \frac{1}{96}}$$

$$\overline{n} = \frac{12}{0.3453}$$

$$\overline{n} = 34.76$$

The critical difference can now be calculated based upon:

$$q_r = 4.62$$

$$MS_{within\ group\ error} = 235.07$$

$$n = 34.76$$

Again, the equation for Tukey's test is:

$$Critical\ difference = q_r \sqrt{\frac{MS_{within\ group\ error}}{n_{(per\ group)}}}$$

$$Critical\ difference = 4.62 \sqrt{\frac{235.07}{34.76}}$$

$$Critical\ difference = 4.62 \times 2.60$$

$$Critical\ difference = 12.015$$

Difference among the 12 means in Interaction ABC

GROUP	Mean	0-1-1	0-1-2	0-2-1	0-2-2	0-3-1	0-3-2	1-1-1	1-1-2	1-2-1	1-2-2	1-3-1	1-3-2
		40.78	54.36	44.16	50.37	46.92	49.9	43.42	46.87	46.76	48.96	45.6	55.67
0-1-1	40.78	–	–13.58	–3.38	–9.59	–6.14	–9.12	–2.64	–6.09	–5.98	–8.18	–4.82	–14.89
0-1-2	54.36	13.58	–	10.2	3.99	7.44	4.46	10.94	7.49	7.6	5.4	8.76	–1.31
0-2-1	44.16	3.38	–10.2	–	–6.21	–2.76	–5.74	0.74	–2.71	–2.6	–4.8	–1.44	–11.51
0-2-2	50.37	9.59	–3.99	6.21	–	3.45	0.47	6.95	3.5	3.61	1.41	4.77	–5.3
0-3-1	46.92	6.14	–7.44	2.76	–3.45	–	–2.98	3.5	0.05	0.16	–2.04	1.32	–8.75
0-3-2	49.9	9.12	–4.46	5.74	–0.47	2.98	–	6.48	3.03	3.14	0.94	4.3	–5.77
1-1-1	43.42	2.64	–10.94	–0.74	–6.95	–3.5	–6.48	–	–3.45	–3.34	–5.54	–2.18	–12.25
1-1-2	46.87	6.09	–7.49	2.71	–3.5	–0.05	–3.03	3.45	–	0.11	–2.09	1.27	–8.8
1-2-1	46.76	5.98	–7.6	2.6	–3.61	–0.16	–3.14	3.34	–0.11	–	–2.2	1.16	–8.91
1-2-2	48.96	8.18	–5.4	4.8	–1.41	2.04	–0.94	5.54	2.09	2.2	–	3.36	–6.71
1-3-1	45.6	4.82	–8.76	1.44	–4.77	–1.32	–4.3	2.18	–1.27	–1.16	–3.36	–	–10.07
1-3-2	55.67	14.89	1.31	11.51	5.3	8.75	5.77	12.25	8.8	8.91	6.71	10.07	–

The group code: Internet (1 = yes, or 0 = no), income (category 1, 2, or 3), and education (category 1 or 2)

Summary: Differences Exceeding the Critical Difference of 12.015 among the 12 means in Interaction ABC

GROUP	Mean	0-1-1	0-1-2	0-2-1	0-2-2	0-3-1	0-3-2	1-1-1	1-1-2	1-2-1	1-2-2	1-3-1	1-3-2
		40.78	54.36	44.16	50.37	46.92	49.9	43.42	46.87	46.76	48.96	45.6	55.67
0-1-1	40.78	–	–13.58	–	–	–	–	–	–	–	–	–	–14.89
0-1-2	54.36	13.58	–	–	–	–	–	–	–	–	–	–	–
0-2-1	44.16	–	–	–	–	–	–	–	–	–	–	–	–
0-2-2	50.37	–	–	–	–	–	–	–	–	–	–	–	–
0-3-1	46.92	–	–	–	–	–	–	–	–	–	–	–	–
0-3-2	49.9	–	–	–	–	–	–	–	–	–	–	–	–
1-1-1	43.42	–	–	–	–	–	–	–	–	–	–	–	–12.25
1-1-2	46.87	–	–	–	–	–	–	–	–	–	–	–	–
1-2-1	46.76	–	–	–	–	–	–	–	–	–	–	–	–
1-2-2	48.96	–	–	–	–	–	–	–	–	–	–	–	–
1-3-1	45.6	–	–	–	–	–	–	–	–	–	–	–	–
1-3-2	55.67	14.89	–	–	–	–	–	12.25	–	–	–	–	–

The group code: Internet (1 = yes, or 0 = no), income (category 1, 2, or 3), and education (category 1 or 2)

APPENDIX L

One-Way ANOVA on Uncategorized Full Set Data

One-Way (Internet access)

Descriptives

NCE total

	N	Mean	Std. Deviation	Std. Error	95% Confidence Interval for Mean		Minimum	Maximum
					Lower Bound	Upper Bound		
0	296	45.25	14.780	.859	43.56	46.94	1	99
1	276	49.36	17.042	1.026	47.34	51.38	1	99
Total	572	47.23	16.030	.670	45.91	48.55	1	99

Test of Homogeneity of Variances

NCE total

Levene Statistic	df1	df2	Sig.
6.836	1	570	.009

ANOVA

NCE total

	Sum of Squares	df	Mean Square	F	Sig.
Between Groups	2415.053	1	2415.053	9.539	.002
Within Groups	144312.5	570	253.180		
Total	146727.5	571			

ONE-WAY AVOVA—INCOME IN SEVEN CATEGORIES

Descriptives

NCE Total Score

					95% Confidence Interval for Mean			
	N	Mean	Std. Deviation	Std. Error	Lower Bound	Upper Bound	Minimum	Maximum
1	88	40.83	14.770	1.575	37.70	43.96	1	74
2	122	45.50	14.163	1.282	42.96	48.04	1	85
3	132	46.67	13.113	1.141	44.42	48.93	1	76
4	54	51.28	19.579	2.664	45.93	56.62	1	99
5	74	43.70	18.447	2.144	39.43	47.98	1	83
6	34	51.03	14.246	2.443	46.06	56.00	27	99
7	68	58.43	14.590	1.769	54.89	61.96	14	90
Total	572	47.23	16.030	.670	45.91	48.55	1	99

Category	Description
1	0–10K
2	10–20K
3	20–30K
4	30–40K
5	40–50K
6	50–60K
7	60K+

Test of Homogeneity of Variances

NCE Total Score

Levene Statistic	df1	df2	Sig.
2.318	6	565	.032

ANOVA

NCE Total Score

	Sum of Squares	df	Mean Square	F	Sig.
Between Groups	14831.707	6	2471.951	10.589	.000
Within Groups	131895.8	565	233.444		
Total	146727.5	571			

POST HOC TESTS—INCOME IN SEVEN CATEGORIES
Multiple Comparisons

Dependent Variable: NCE Total Score
Scheffe

					95% Confidence Interval	
(I) Income	(J) Income	Mean Difference (I–J)	Std. Error	Sig.	Lower Bound	Upper Bound
1	2	−4.670	2.137	.573	−12.28	2.94
	3	−5.845	2.103	.261	−13.33	1.65
	4	−10.448*	2.641	.017	−19.86	−1.04
	5	−2.873	2.410	.964	−11.46	5.71
	6	−10.200	3.085	.093	−21.19	.79
	7	−17.597*	2.467	.000	−26.38	−8.81
2	1	4.670	2.137	.573	−2.94	12.28
	3	−1.174	1.919	.999	−8.01	5.66
	4	−5.778	2.497	.500	−14.67	3.12
	5	1.797	2.251	.996	−6.22	9.82

(Continued)

Appendix

Table *(Continued)*

(I) Income	(J) Income	Mean Difference (I–J)	Std. Error	Sig.	95% Confidence Interval Lower Bound	Upper Bound
	6	−5.529	2.963	.746	−16.08	5.02
	7	−12.926*	2.312	.000	−21.16	−4.69
3	1	5.845	2.103	.261	−1.65	13.33
	2	1.174	1.919	.999	−5.66	8.01
	4	−4.604	2.468	.747	−13.39	4.19
	5	2.972	2.219	.937	−4.93	10.87
	6	−4.355	2.938	.900	−14.82	6.11
	7	−11.752*	2.281	.000	−19.88	−3.63
4	1	10.448*	2.641	.017	1.04	19.86
	2	5.778	2.497	.500	−3.12	14.67
	3	4.604	2.468	.747	−4.19	13.39
	5	7.575	2.735	.265	−2.17	17.32
	6	.248	3.345	1.000	−11.67	12.16
	7	−7.149	2.785	.362	−17.07	2.77
5	1	2.873	2.410	.964	−5.71	11.46
	2	−1.797	2.251	.996	−9.82	6.22
	3	−2.972	2.219	.937	−10.87	4.93
	4	−7.575	2.735	.265	−17.32	2.17
	6	−7.327	3.166	.500	−18.60	3.95
	7	−14.724*	2.567	.000	−23.87	−5.58
6	1	10.200	3.085	.093	−.79	21.19
	2	5.529	2.963	.746	−5.02	16.08
	3	4.355	2.938	.900	−6.11	14.82
	4	−.248	3.345	1.000	−12.16	11.67
	5	7.327	3.166	.500	−3.95	18.60
	7	−7.397	3.209	.505	−18.83	4.03
7	1	17.597*	2.467	.000	8.81	26.38
	2	12.926*	2.312	.000	4.69	21.16
	3	11.752*	2.281	.000	3.63	19.88
	4	7.149	2.785	.362	−2.77	17.07
	5	14.724*	2.567	.000	5.58	23.87
	6	7.397	3.209	.505	−4.03	18.83

* The mean difference is significant at the .05 level.

ONE-WAY ANOVA EDUCATION IN SIX CATEGORIES

Category	Description
1	Finished Elementary School
2	Graduated from High School
3	Attended College or training after High School
4	Completed a 2-year college or training program
5	Completed a 4-year degree at a college or University
6	Attended or completed a College Graduate Program

Descriptives

NCE Total Score

	N	Mean	Std. Deviation	Std. Error	95% Confidence Interval for Mean		Minimum	Maximum
					Lower Bound	Upper Bound		
1	12	46.00	15.556	4.491	36.12	55.88	1	63
2	99	41.48	16.151	1.623	38.26	44.71	1	92
3	120	42.21	15.092	1.378	39.48	44.94	1	76
4	102	46.90	14.288	1.415	44.10	49.71	1	99
5	100	50.66	15.542	1.554	47.58	53.74	3	85
6	139	53.54	15.658	1.328	50.91	56.17	14	99
Total	572	47.23	16.030	.670	45.91	48.55	1	99

Test of Homogeneity of Variances

NCE Total Score

Levene Statistic	df1	df2	Sig.
.707	5	566	.618

Appendix

ANOVA

NCE Total Score

	Sum of Squares	df	Mean Square	F	Sig.
Between Groups	13033.028	5	2606.606	11.035	.000
Within Groups	133694.5	566	236.209		
Total	146727.5	571			

Multiple Comparisons

Dependent Variable: NCE Total Score Scheffe

					95% Confidence Interval	
(I) Education	(J) Education	Mean Difference (I–J)	Std. Error	Sig.	Lower Bound	Upper Bound
1	2	4.515	4.698	.968	−11.17	20.20
	3	3.792	4.653	.985	−11.75	19.33
	4	−.902	4.690	1.000	−16.56	14.76
	5	−4.660	4.695	.964	−20.34	11.02
	6	−7.540	4.624	.752	−22.98	7.90
2	1	−4.515	4.698	.968	−20.20	11.17
	3	−.723	2.087	1.000	−7.69	6.24
	4	−5.417	2.168	.285	−12.66	1.82
	5	−9.175*	2.179	.004	−16.45	−1.90
	6	−12.055*	2.021	.000	−18.80	−5.31
3	1	−3.792	4.653	.985	−19.33	11.75
	2	.723	2.087	1.000	−6.24	7.69
	4	−4.694	2.070	.400	−11.61	2.22
	5	−8.452*	2.081	.006	−15.40	−1.50
	6	−11.331*	1.915	.000	−17.73	−4.94
4	1	.902	4.690	1.000	−14.76	16.56
	2	5.417	2.168	.285	−1.82	12.66
	3	4.694	2.070	.400	−2.22	11.61
	5	−3.758	2.163	.697	−10.98	3.46
	6	−6.638	2.004	.053	−13.33	.05

(Continued)

TABLE *(Continued)*

(I) Education	(J) Education	Mean Difference (I–J)	Std. Error	Sig.	95% Confidence Interval	
					Lower Bound	Upper Bound
5	1	4.660	4.695	.964	−11.02	20.34
	2	9.175*	2.179	.004	1.90	16.45
	3	8.452*	2.081	.006	1.50	15.40
	4	3.758	2.163	.697	−3.46	10.98
	6	−2.880	2.015	.843	−9.61	3.85
6	1	7.540	4.624	.752	−7.90	22.98
	2	12.055*	2.021	.000	5.31	18.80
	3	11.331*	1.915	.000	4.94	17.73
	4	6.638	2.004	.053	−.05	13.33
	5	2.880	2.015	.843	−3.85	9.61

* The mean difference is significant at the .05 level.

APPENDIX M

ONE-WAY ANOVA

ON CATEGORIZED FULL SET DATA

ONE-WAY—INCOME IN THREE CATEGORIES

Descriptives

NCE total

	N	Mean	Std. Deviation	Std. Error	95% Confidence Interval for Mean		Minimum	Maximum
					Lower Bound	Upper Bound		
1	210	43.54	14.570	1.005	41.56	45.52	1	85
2	132	46.67	13.113	1.141	44.42	48.93	1	76
3	230	50.92	17.953	1.184	48.58	53.25	1	99
Total	572	47.23	16.030	.670	45.91	48.55	1	99

Test of Homogeneity of Variances

NCE total

Levene Statistic	df1	df2	Sig.
6.663	2	569	.001

ANOVA

NCE total

	Sum of Squares	df	Mean Square	F	Sig.
Between Groups	6023.001	2	3011.501	12.178	.000
Within Groups	140704.5	569	247.284		
Total	146727.5	571			

POST HOC TESTS—INCOME IN THREE CATEGORIES

Multiple Comparisons

Dependent Variable: NCE total

	INCOME (I)	INCOME (J)	Mean Difference (I–J)	Std. Error	Sig.	95% Confidence Interval Lower Bound	95% Confidence Interval Upper Bound
Scheffe	1	2	−3.13	1.747	.201	−7.42	1.16
		3	−7.37*	1.501	.000	−11.06	−3.69
	2	1	3.13	1.747	.201	−1.16	7.42
		3	−4.24*	1.717	.048	−8.46	−.03
	3	1	7.37*	1.501	.000	3.69	11.06
		2	4.24*	1.717	.048	.03	8.46

* The mean difference is significant at the .05 level.

ONE-WAY (EDUCATION)

Descriptives

NCE total

	N	Mean	Std. Deviation	Std. Error	95% Confidence Interval for Mean		Minimum	Maximum
					Lower Bound	Upper Bound		
1	333	43.57	15.308	.839	41.92	45.22	1	99
2	239	52.33	15.642	1.012	50.34	54.33	3	99
Total	572	47.23	16.030	.670	45.91	48.55	1	99

Test of Homogeneity of Variances

NCE total

Levene Statistic	df1	df2	Sig.
.789	1	570	.375

ANOVA

NCE total

	Sum of Squares	df	Mean Square	F	Sig.
Between Groups	10694.587	1	10694.587	44.812	.000
Within Groups	136033.0	570	238.654		
Total	146727.5	571			

APPENDIX N

ANALYSIS: FIRST TRIMMED DATASET

UNIVARIATE ANALYSIS OF VARIANCE

Between-Subjects Factors

		N
INTERNET	0	290
	1	270
INCOME	1	206
	2	131
	3	223
Education	1	323
	2	237

Levene's Test of Equality of Error Variances[a]

Dependent Variable: NCE total

F	df1	df2	Sig.
2.009	11	548	.026

Tests the null hypothesis that the error variance of the dependent variable is equal across groups.

[a] Design: Intercept + INTERNET + INCOME + EDUCATION + INTERNET *INCOME + INTERNET * EDUCATION + INCOME * EDUCATION + INTERNET * INCOME * EDUCATION

Descriptive Statistics

Dependent Variable: NCE total

INTERNET	INCOME	Education	Mean	Std. Deviation	N
0	1	1	41.77	12.201	121
		2	54.36	14.688	25
		Total	43.92	13.474	146
	2	1	45.02	12.298	50
		2	50.37	8.858	19
		Total	46.49	11.642	69
	3	1	44.75	12.095	24
		2	48.94	14.740	51
		Total	47.60	14.005	75
	Total	1	42.97	12.247	195
		2	50.65	13.818	95
		Total	45.49	13.261	290
1	1	1	44.57	14.381	37
		2	46.87	11.760	23
		Total	45.45	13.380	60
	2	1	46.76	14.325	38
		2	48.96	12.338	24
		Total	47.61	13.529	62
	3	1	48.96	15.347	53
		2	55.21	17.063	95
		Total	52.97	16.689	148
	Total	1	47.04	14.771	128
		2	52.80	15.896	142
		Total	50.07	15.613	270
Total	1	1	42.42	12.752	158
		2	50.77	13.755	48
		Total	44.37	13.432	206
	2	1	45.77	13.161	88
		2	49.58	10.839	43
		Total	47.02	12.534	131

(Continued)

TABLE *(Continued)*

INTERNET	INCOME	Education	Mean	Std. Deviation	N
	3	1	47.65	14.467	77
		2	53.02	16.512	146
		Total	51.17	16.009	223
	Total	1	44.58	13.432	323
		2	51.94	15.104	237
		Total	47.70	14.611	560

Tests of Between-Subjects Effects

Dependent Variable: NCE total

Source	Type III Sum of Squares	df	Mean Square	F	Sig.	Partial Eta Squared	Noncent. Parameter	Observed Power[a]
Corrected Model	12041.157[b]	11	1094.651	5.591	.000	.101	61.502	1.000
Intercept	949565.806	1	949565.806	4850.086	.000	.898	4850.086	1.000
INTERNET	107.109	1	107.109	.547	.460	.001	.547	.114
INCOME	533.819	2	266.909	1.363	.257	.005	2.727	.294
EDUCATION	3087.708	1	3087.708	15.771	.000	.028	15.771	.977
INTERNET * INCOME	1165.974	2	582.987	2.978	.052	.011	5.955	.578
INTERNET * EDUCATION	370.319	1	370.319	1.891	.170	.003	1.891	.279
INCOME * EDUCATION	215.904	2	107.952	.551	.576	.002	1.103	.141
INTERNET * INCOME * EDUCATION	727.926	2	363.963	1.859	.157	.007	3.718	.388
Error	107289.236	548	195.783					
Total	1393302.000	560						
Corrected Total	119330.393	559						

[a] Computed using alpha = .05.
[b] R Squared = .101 (Adjusted R Squared = .083).

ESTIMATED MARGINAL MEANS

1. Grand Mean

Dependent Variable: NCE total

Mean	Std. Error	95% Confidence Interval	
		Lower Bound	Upper Bound
48.045	.690	46.690	49.400

2. INTERNET

Dependent Variable: NCE total

INTERNET	Mean	Std. Error	95% Confidence Interval	
			Lower Bound	Upper Bound
0	47.535	.995	45.580	49.490
1	48.555	.956	46.678	50.432

3. INCOME

Dependent Variable: NCE total

INCOME	Mean	Std. Error	95% Confidence Interval	
			Lower Bound	Upper Bound
1	46.891	1.206	44.523	49.259
2	47.777	1.312	45.201	50.354
3	49.466	1.053	47.397	51.535

4. Education

Dependent Variable: NCE total

Education	Mean	Std. Error	95% Confidence Interval	
			Lower Bound	Upper Bound
1	45.305	.879	43.578	47.032
2	50.785	1.063	48.696	52.873

5. INTERNET * INCOME

Dependent Variable: NCE total

INTERNET	INCOME	Mean	Std. Error	95% Confidence Interval	
				Lower Bound	Upper Bound
0	1	48.064	1.537	45.045	51.083
	2	47.694	1.885	43.991	51.398
	3	46.846	1.732	43.444	50.247
1	1	45.719	1.858	42.070	49.368
	2	47.861	1.824	44.278	51.444
	3	52.086	1.199	49.730	54.443

6. INTERNET * Education

Dependent Variable: NCE total

INTERNET	Education	Mean	Std. Error	95% Confidence Interval	
				Lower Bound	Upper Bound
0	1	43.846	1.233	41.423	46.269
	2	51.223	1.563	48.154	54.293
1	1	46.764	1.253	44.302	49.226
	2	50.346	1.443	47.512	53.180

7. INCOME * Education

Dependent Variable: NCE total

| | | | | 95% Confidence Interval | |
INCOME	Education	Mean	Std. Error	Lower Bound	Upper Bound
1	1	43.168	1.314	40.586	45.750
	2	50.615	2.021	46.644	54.585
2	1	45.892	1.506	42.934	48.849
	2	49.663	2.148	45.443	53.883
3	1	46.856	1.721	43.475	50.237
	2	52.076	1.214	49.690	54.461

8. INTERNET * INCOME * Education

Dependent Variable: NCE total

| | | | | | 95% Confidence Interval | |
INTERNET	INCOME	Education	Mean	Std. Error	Lower Bound	Upper Bound
0	1	1	41.769	1.272	39.270	44.267
		2	54.360	2.798	48.863	59.857
	2	1	45.020	1.979	41.133	48.907
		2	50.368	3.210	44.063	56.674
	3	1	44.750	2.856	39.140	50.360
		2	48.941	1.959	45.093	52.790
1	1	1	44.568	2.300	40.049	49.086
		2	46.870	2.918	41.139	52.601
	2	1	46.763	2.270	42.304	51.222
		2	48.958	2.856	43.348	54.569
	3	1	48.962	1.922	45.187	52.738
		2	55.211	1.436	52.391	58.030

Appendix

Post Hoc Tests—INCOME

Multiple Comparisons

Dependent Variable: NCE total

	INCOME (I)	INCOME (J)	Mean Difference (I–J)	Std. Error	Sig.	95% Confidence Interval Lower Bound	Upper Bound
Scheffe	1	2	−2.65	1.564	.238	−6.49	1.18
		3	−6.80*	1.352	.000	−10.12	−3.48
	2	1	2.65	1.564	.238	−1.18	6.49
		3	−4.14*	1.540	.027	−7.92	−.36
	3	1	6.80*	1.352	.000	3.48	10.12
		2	4.14*	1.540	.027	.36	7.92
LSD	1	2	−2.65	1.564	.090	−5.73	.42
		3	−6.80*	1.352	.000	−9.45	−4.14
	2	1	2.65	1.564	.090	−.42	5.73
		3	−4.14*	1.540	.007	−7.17	−1.12
	3	1	6.80*	1.352	.000	4.14	9.45
		2	4.14*	1.540	.007	1.12	7.17
Dunnett T3	1	2	−2.65	1.441	.186	−6.11	.80
		3	−6.80*	1.423	.000	−10.21	−3.39
	2	1	2.65	1.441	.186	−.80	6.11
		3	−4.14*	1.532	.021	−7.82	−.47
	3	1	6.80*	1.423	.000	3.39	10.21
		2	4.14*	1.532	.021	.47	7.82

Based on observed means.
* The mean difference is significant at the .05 level.

HOMOGENEOUS SUBSETS

NCE total

	INCOME	N	Subset 1	Subset 2
Student-Newman-Keuls[a,c]	1	206	44.37	
	2	131	47.02	
	3	223		51.17
	Sig.		.075	1.000
Scheffe[a,b,c]	1	206	44.37	
	2	131	47.02	
	3	223		51.17
	Sig.		.205	1.000

Means for groups in homogeneous subsets are displayed.
Based on Type III Sum of Squares
The error term is Mean Square (Error) = 195.783.
[a] Uses Harmonic Mean Sample Size = 176.759.
[b] The group sizes are unequal. The harmonic mean of the group sizes is used. Type I error levels are not guaranteed.
[c] Alpha = .05.

APPENDIX O

UNBALANCED FACTORIAL ANOVA

UNIVARIATE ANALYSIS OF VARIANCE

Between-Subjects Factors

		N
INTERNET	0	289
	1	267
INCOME	1	206
	2	131
	3	219
Education	1	321
	2	235

Levene's Test of Equality of Error Variances[a]

Dependent Variable: NCE total

F	df1	df2	Sig.
1.794	11	544	.052

Tests the null hypothesis that the error variance of
the dependent variable is equal across groups.
[a] Design: Intercept + INTERNET + INCOME + EDUCATION + INTERNET
* INCOME + INTERNET * EDUCATION + INCOME
*EDUCATION + INTERNET * INCOME * EDUCATION

Descriptive Statistics

Dependent Variable: NCE total

INTERNET	INCOME	Education	Mean	Std. Deviation	N
0	1	1	41.77	12.201	121
		2	54.36	14.688	25
		Total	43.92	13.474	146
	2	1	45.02	12.298	50
		2	50.37	8.858	19
		Total	46.49	11.642	69
	3	1	44.75	12.095	24
		2	49.86	13.332	50
		Total	48.20	13.085	74
	Total	1	42.97	12.247	195
		2	51.16	12.973	94
		Total	45.63	13.045	289
1	1	1	44.57	14.381	37
		2	46.87	11.760	23
		Total	45.45	13.380	60
	2	1	46.76	14.325	38
		2	48.96	12.338	24
		Total	47.61	13.529	62
	3	1	47.27	12.960	51
		2	55.77	16.268	94
		Total	52.78	15.678	145
	Total	1	46.33	13.742	126
		2	53.16	15.383	141
		Total	49.93	14.998	267
Total	1	1	42.42	12.752	158
		2	50.77	13.755	48
		Total	44.37	13.432	206
	2	1	45.77	13.161	88
		2	49.58	10.839	43
		Total	47.02	12.534	131
	3	1	46.47	12.663	75
		2	53.72	15.524	144
		Total	51.23	14.980	219
	Total	1	44.29	12.938	321
		2	52.36	14.472	235
		Total	47.70	14.168	556

Tests of Between-Subjects Effects

Dependent Variable: NCE total

Source	Type III Sum of Squares	df	Mean Square	F	Sig.	Partial Eta Squared	Noncent. Parameter	Observed Power[a]
Corrected Model	12877.511[b]	11	1170.683	6.463	.000	.116	71.098	1.000
Intercept	945502.428	1	945502.428	5220.180	.000	.906	5220.180	1.000
INTERNET	47.202	1	47.202	.261	.610	.000	.261	.080
INCOME	506.547	2	253.273	1.398	.248	.005	2.797	.301
EDUCATION	3697.074	1	3697.074	20.412	.000	.036	20.412	.995
INTERNET * INCOME	846.531	2	423.265	2.337	.098	.009	4.674	.473
INTERNET * EDUCATION	288.155	1	288.155	1.591	.208	.003	1.591	.242
INCOME * EDUCATION	235.768	2	117.884	.651	.522	.002	1.302	.159
INTERNET * INCOME * EDUCATION	888.772	2	444.386	2.453	.087	.009	4.907	.493
Error	98531.726	544	181.124					
Total	1376356.000	556						
Corrected Total	111409.237	555						

a Computed using alpha = .05.
b R Squared = .116 (Adjusted R Squared = .09840).

ESTIMATED MARGINAL MEANS

1. Grand Mean

Dependent Variable: NCE total

Mean	Std. Error	95% Confidence Interval	
		Lower Bound	Upper Bound
48.027	.665	46.721	49.333

2. INTERNET

Dependent Variable: NCE total

INTERNET	Mean	Std. Error	95% Confidence Interval	
			Lower Bound	Upper Bound
0	47.688	.958	45.805	49.570
1	48.367	.921	46.557	50.176

3. INCOME

Dependent Variable: NCE total

INCOME	Mean	Std. Error	95% Confidence Interval	
			Lower Bound	Upper Bound
1	46.891	1.160	44.614	49.169
2	47.777	1.262	45.299	50.256
3	49.413	1.020	47.409	51.416

4. Education

Dependent Variable: NCE total

Education	Mean	Std. Error	95% Confidence Interval	
			Lower Bound	Upper Bound
1	45.024	.848	43.358	46.689
2	51.030	1.024	49.019	53.042

5. INTERNET * INCOME

Dependent Variable: NCE total

INTERNET	INCOME	Mean	Std. Error	95% Confidence Interval	
				Lower Bound	Upper Bound
0	1	48.064	1.478	45.160	50.968
	2	47.694	1.814	44.132	51.257
	3	47.305	1.671	44.023	50.587
1	1	45.719	1.787	42.209	49.228
	2	47.861	1.755	44.414	51.307
	3	51.520	1.170	49.221	53.819

6. INTERNET * Education

Dependent Variable: NCE total

INTERNET	Education	Mean	Std. Error	95% Confidence Interval	
				Lower Bound	Upper Bound
0	1	43.846	1.186	41.516	46.177
	2	51.529	1.506	48.572	54.487
1	1	46.202	1.212	43.822	48.582
	2	50.531	1.388	47.804	53.259

7. INCOME * Education

Dependent Variable: NCE total

				95% Confidence Interval	
INCOME	Education	Mean	Std. Error	Lower Bound	Upper Bound
1	1	43.168	1.264	40.685	45.651
	2	50.615	1.944	46.796	54.434
2	1	45.892	1.448	43.047	48.736
	2	49.663	2.066	45.604	53.722
3	1	46.012	1.666	42.740	49.284
	2	52.813	1.178	50.499	55.127

8. INTERNET * INCOME * Education

Dependent Variable: NCE total

					95% Confidence Interval	
INTERNET	INCOME	Education	Mean	Std. Error	Lower Bound	Upper Bound
0	1	1	41.769	1.223	39.365	44.172
		2	54.360	2.692	49.073	59.647
	2	1	45.020	1.903	41.281	48.759
		2	50.368	3.088	44.303	56.433
	3	1	44.750	2.747	39.354	50.146
		2	49.860	1.903	46.121	53.599
1	1	1	44.568	2.213	40.221	48.914
		2	46.870	2.806	41.357	52.382
	2	1	46.763	2.183	42.475	51.052
		2	48.958	2.747	43.562	54.355
	3	1	47.275	1.885	43.573	50.976
		2	55.766	1.388	53.039	58.493

Post Hoc Tests—INCOME

Multiple Comparisons

Dependent Variable: NCE total

	INCOME (I)	INCOME (J)	Mean Difference (I–J)	Std. Error	Sig.	95% Confidence Interval Lower Bound	Upper Bound
Scheffe	1	2	−2.65	1.504	.212	−6.35	1.04
		3	−6.86*	1.306	.000	−10.07	−3.66
	2	1	2.65	1.504	.212	−1.04	6.35
		3	−4.21*	1.486	.019	−7.86	−.56
	3	1	6.86*	1.306	.000	3.66	10.07
		2	4.21*	1.486	.019	.56	7.86
LSD	1	2	−2.65	1.504	.078	−5.61	.30
		3	−6.86*	1.306	.000	−9.43	−4.30
	2	1	2.65	1.504	.078	−.30	5.61
		3	−4.21*	1.486	.005	−7.13	−1.29
	3	1	6.86*	1.306	.000	4.30	9.43
		2	4.21*	1.486	.005	1.29	7.13
Dunnett T3	1	2	−2.65	1.441	.186	−6.11	.80
		3	−6.86*	1.379	.000	−10.17	−3.56
	2	1	2.65	1.441	.186	−.80	6.11
		3	−4.21*	1.491	.015	−7.79	−.63
	3	1	6.86*	1.379	.000	3.56	10.17
		2	4.21*	1.491	.015	.63	7.79

Based on observed means.
* The mean difference is significant at the .05 level.

HOMOGENEOUS SUBSETS

NCE TOTAL

	INCOME	N	Subset 1	Subset 2
Student-Newman-Keuls[a,b]	1	206	44.37	
	2	131	47.02	
	3	219		51.23
	Sig.		.065	1.000
Scheffe[a,b,c]	1	206	44.37	
	2	131	47.02	
	3	219		51.23
	Sig.		.182	1.000

Means for groups in homogeneous subsets are displayed.
Based on Type III Sum of Squares
The error term is Mean Square (Error) = 181.124.
[a] Harmonic Mean Sample Size = 175.910.
[b] The group sizes are unequal. The harmonic mean of the group sizes is used. Type I error levels are not guaranteed.
[c] Alpha = .05.

APPENDIX P

Unbalanced Interaction Graphs
for Factors A & B

Unbalanced AB Interaction Data: Internet & Income, on NCE Total Scale

Internet	No	Yes	No	Yes	No	Yes
Income Category	1	1	2	2	3	3
Mean	48.06	45.72	47.69	47.86	47.31	51.52
N	146	60	69	62	75	148

Unbalanced Interaction Chart: Internet & Income, on NCE Total Scale

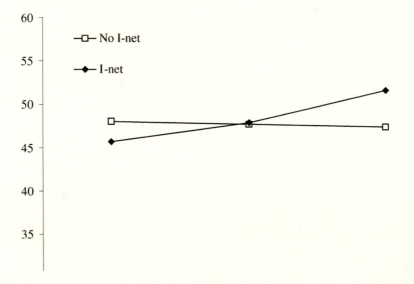

Unbalanced Interaction Chart Data: Internet & Income, on NCE Total Scale

	0–20K	20–30K	30K+
No I-net	48.06	47.69	47.31
I-net	45.72	47.86	51.52

Unbalanced Interaction Chart: Income & Internet, on NCE Total Scale

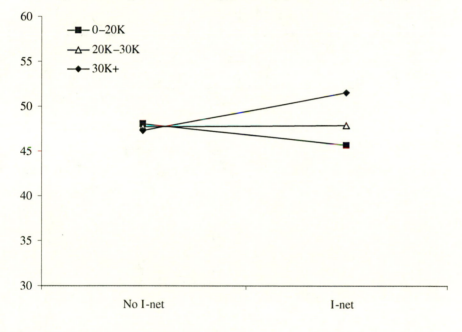

Unbalanced Interaction Chart Data: Income & Internet, on NCE Total Scale

	No I-net	I-net
0–20K	48.06	45.75
20–30K	47.69	47.86
30k+	47.31	51.52

APPENDIX Q

Unbalanced Interaction Graphs
for Factors A & C

Unbalanced AC Interaction Data: Internet & Education, on NCE Total Scale

Internet	No	Yes	No	Yes
Education Category	1	1	2	2
Mean	43.85	46.20	51.53	50.53
N	195	126	94	141

Unbalanced Interaction Chart: Internet & Education, on NCE Total Scale

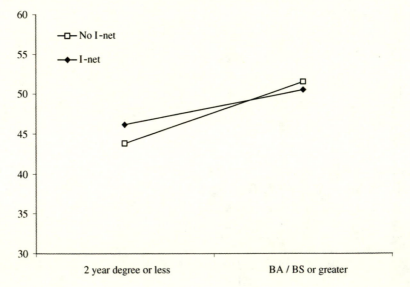

Unbalanced Interaction Chart Data: Internet &
Education, on NCE Total Scale

	2 year degree or less	BA / BS or greater
No I-net	43.85	51.53
I-net	46.20	50.53

Unbalanced Interaction Chart: Education & Internet, on NCE Total Scale

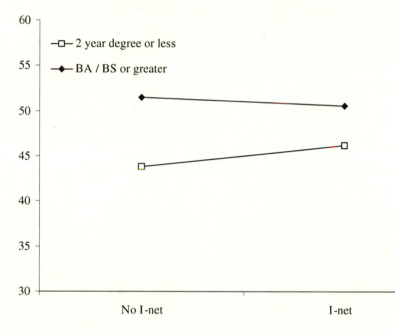

Unbalanced Interaction Chart Data: Education &
Internet, on NCE Total Scale

	No I-net	I-net
2-year degree or less	43.85	46.20
BA / BS or greater	51.53	50.53

APPENDIX R

UNBALANCED INTERACTION GRAPHS FOR FACTORS B & C

Unbalanced BC Interaction Data: Income & Education, on NCE Total Scale

Income Category	1	1	2	2	3	3
Education Category	1	2	1	2	1	2
Mean	43.17	50.61	45.89	49.66	46.01	52.81
N	158	48	88	43	75	144

Unbalanced Interaction Chart: Income & Education, on NCE Total Scale

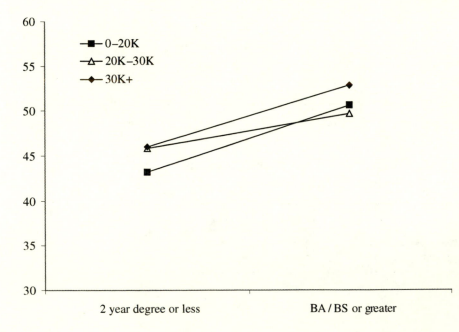

Unbalanced Interaction Chart Data: Income &
Education, on NCE Total Scale

	2 year degree or less	BA / BS or greater
0–20K	43.17	50.61
20–30K	45.89	49.66
30k+	46.01	52.81

Unbalanced Interaction Chart: Education & Income, on NCE
Total Scale

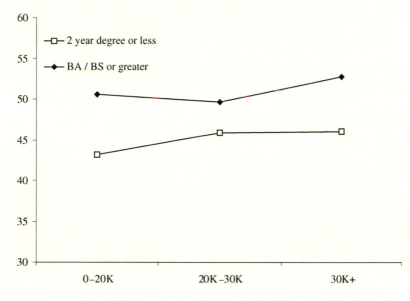

Interaction Chart Data: Education & Income,
on NCE Total Scale

	0–20K	20–30K	30K+
2 year degree or less	43.17	45.89	46.01
BA / BS or greater	50.61	49.66	52.81

APPENDIX S

UNBALANCED INTERACTION GRAPHS FOR FACTORS A & B & C

Unbalanced ABC Interaction Data: Internet, Income & Education, on NCE Total Scale

Internet	TRUE			FALSE		
Income	0–20K	20–30K	30K+	0–20K	20–30K	30K+
Elementary School—High School—Some College—2-year degree	44.57	46.76	47.27	41.77	45.02	44.75
4-year degree—Graduate Program	46.87	48.96	55.77	54.36	50.37	49.86

Unbalanced Interaction Chart: Internet, Income & Education, on NCE Total Scale

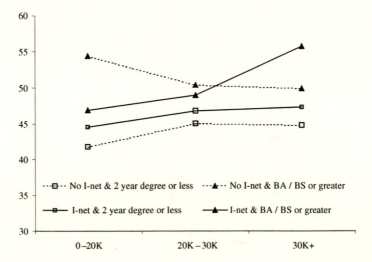

Unbalanced Interaction Chart Data: Internet, Income &
Education, on NCE Total Scale

	0–20K	20–30K	30K+
No I-net & 2 year degree or less	41.77	45.02	44.75
No I-net & BA / BS or greater	54.36	50.37	49.86
I-net & 2 year degree or less	44.57	46.76	47.27
I-net & BA / BS or greater	46.87	48.96	55.77

Unbalanced Interaction Chart: Internet, Income & Education, on NCE
Total Scale

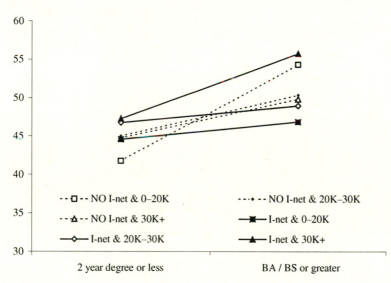

Unbalanced Interaction Chart Data: Internet, Income & Education, on NCE Total Scale

	2 year degree or less	BA/BS or greater
NO I-net & 0–20K	41.77	54.36
NO I-net & 20–30K	45.02	50.37
NO I-net & 30k+	44.75	49.86
I-net & 0–20K	44.57	46.87
I-net & 20–30K	46.76	48.96
I-net & 30k+	47.27	55.77

Unbalanced Interaction Chart: Internet, Income & Education, on NCE Total Scale

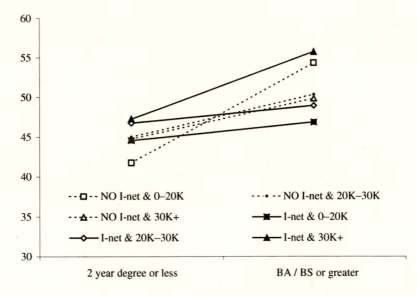

Interaction Chart Data: Internet, Income & Education, on NCE Total Scale

	No-Internet at home	Internet at home
Less than BS & $0–20K	41.77	54.36
More than BS & $0–20K	45.02	50.37
Less than BS & $20–30K	44.75	49.86
More than BS & $20–30K	44.57	46.87
Less than BS & $30k+	46.76	48.96
More than BS & $30k+	47.27	55.77

APPENDIX T

ONE-WAY ANOVA FOR FACTORS A, B, & C

ONE-WAY ANOVA FOR FACTOR A (INTERNET)

Descriptives

NCE total

	N	Mean	Std. Deviation	Std. Error	95% Confidence Interval for Mean Lower Bound	95% Confidence Interval for Mean Upper Bound	Minimum	Maximum
0	289	45.63	13.045	.767	44.12	47.14	8	85
1	267	49.93	14.998	.918	48.13	51.74	5	90
Total	556	47.70	14.168	.601	46.52	48.88	5	90

Test of Homogeneity of Variances

NCE total

Levene Statistic	df1	df2	Sig.
7.389	1	554	.007

ANOVA

NCE total

	Sum of Squares	df	Mean Square	F	Sig.
Between Groups	2565.330	1	2565.330	13.057	.000
Within Groups	108843.9	554	196.469		
Total	111409.2	555			

ONE-WAY ANOVA FOR FACTOR B (INCOME)

Descriptives

NCE total

	N	Mean	Std. Deviation	Std. Error	95% Confidence Interval for Mean		Minimum	Maximum
					Lower Bound	Upper Bound		
1	206	44.37	13.432	.936	42.52	46.21	5	85
2	131	47.02	12.534	1.095	44.86	49.19	16	76
3	219	51.23	14.980	1.012	49.24	53.23	14	90
Total	556	47.70	14.168	.601	46.52	48.88	5	90

Test of Homogeneity of Variances

NCE total

Levene Statistic	df1	df2	Sig.
3.375	2	553	.035

ANOVA

NCE total

	Sum of Squares	df	Mean Square	F	Sig.
Between Groups	5079.222	2	2539.611	13.208	.000
Within Groups	106330.0	553	192.279		
Total	111409.2	555			

Post Hoc Tests

Multiple Comparisons

Dependent Variable: NCE total

	(I) INCOME	(J) INCOME	Mean Difference (I-J)	Std. Error	Sig.	95% Confidence Interval	
						Lower Bound	Upper Bound
Scheffe	1	2	–2.65	1.550	.232	–6.46	1.15
		3	–6.86*	1.346	.000	–10.17	–3.56
	2	1	2.65	1.550	.232	–1.15	6.46
		3	–4.21*	1.532	.023	–7.97	–.45
	3	1	6.86*	1.346	.000	3.56	10.17
		2	4.21*	1.532	.023	.45	7.97
LSD	1	2	–2.65	1.550	.087	–5.70	.39
		3	–6.86*	1.346	.000	–9.51	–4.22
	2	1	2.65	1.550	.087	–.39	5.70
		3	–4.21*	1.532	.006	–7.22	–1.20
	3	1	6.86*	1.346	.000	4.22	9.51
		2	4.21*	1.532	.006	1.20	7.22
Dunnett T3	1	2	–2.65	1.441	.186	–6.11	.80
		3	–6.86*	1.379	.000	–10.17	-3.56
	2	1	2.65	1.441	.186	–.80	6.11
		3	–4.21*	1.491	.015	–7.79	–.63
	3	1	6.86*	1.379	.000	3.56	10.17
		2	4.21*	1.491	.015	.63	7.79

* The mean difference is significant at the .05 level.

HOMOGENEOUS SUBSETS
NCE total

| | INCOME | N | Subset for alpha = .05 | |
			1	2
Student-Newman-Keuls[a,b]	1	206	44.37	
	2	131	47.02	
	3	219		51.23
	Sig.		.073	1.000
Scheffe[a,b]	1	206	44.37	
	2	131	47.02	
	3	219		51.23
	Sig.		.201	1.000

Means for groups in homogeneous subsets are displayed.

[a] Uses Harmonic Mean Sample Size = 175.910. a.

[b] The group sizes are unequal. The harmonic mean of the group sizes is used. Type I error levels are not guaranteed.

ONE-WAY ANOVA FOR FACTOR C (EDUCATION)

Descriptives

NCE total

| | N | Mean | Std. Deviation | Std. Error | 95% Confidence Interval for | | Minimum | Maximum |
					Lower Bound	Upper Bound		
1	321	44.29	12.938	.722	42.87	45.71	5	76
2	235	52.36	14.472	.944	50.50	54.22	14	90
Total	556	47.70	14.168	.601	46.52	48.88	5	90

Test of Homogeneity of Variances

NCE total

Levene Statistic	df1	df2	Sig.
3.983	1	554	.046

Appendix

ANOVA

NCE total

	Sum of Squares	df	Mean Square	F	Sig.
Between Groups	8837.631	1	8837.631	47.733	.000
Within Groups	102571.6	554	185.147		
Total	111409.2	555			

APPENDIX U

FULLY CROSSED AND BALANCED A & B & C FACTORIAL ANOVA

UNIVARIATE ANALYSIS OF VARIANCE

Between-Subjects Factors

		N
INTERNET	0	114
	1	114
INCOME	1	76
	2	76
	3	76
Education	1	114
	2	114

Levene's Test of Equality of Error Variancesa

Dependent Variable: NCE

F	df1	df2	Sig.
1.248	11	216	.257

Tests the null hypothesis that the error variance of the dependent variable is equal across groups.

a Design:
Intercept+INTERNET+INCOME+EDUCATIO+INTERNET
∗ INCOME+INTERNET ∗ EDUCATIO+INCOME ∗
EDUCATIO+INTERNET ∗ INCOME ∗ EDUCATIO

Descriptive Statistics

Dependent Variable: NCE

INTERNET	INCOME	Education	Mean	Std. Deviation	N
0	1	1	40.84	12.549	19
		2	54.42	14.968	19
		Total	47.63	15.262	38
	2	1	45.32	12.356	19
		2	50.37	8.858	19
		Total	47.84	10.909	38
	3	1	45.95	11.759	19
		2	49.84	15.872	19
		Total	47.89	13.918	38
	Total	1	44.04	12.223	57
		2	51.54	13.508	57
		Total	47.79	13.367	114
1	1	1	45.58	13.385	19
		2	46.32	13.204	19
		Total	45.95	13.119	38
	2	1	47.37	14.664	19
		2	49.05	12.295	19
		Total	48.21	13.374	38
	3	1	47.89	14.479	19
		2	56.74	16.865	19
		Total	52.32	16.138	38
	Total	1	46.95	13.967	57
		2	50.70	14.692	57
		Total	48.82	14.395	114
Total	1	1	43.21	13.020	38
		2	50.37	14.515	38
		Total	46.79	14.161	76
	2	1	46.34	13.415	38
		2	49.71	10.590	38
		Total	48.03	12.124	76
	3	1	46.92	13.047	38
		2	53.29	16.527	38
		Total	50.11	15.133	76
	Total	1	45.49	13.147	114
		2	51.12	14.056	114
		Total	48.31	13.870	228

Tests of Between-Subjects Effects

Dependent Variable: NCE

Source	Type III Sum of Squares	df	Mean Square	F	Sig.	Partial Eta Squared	Noncent. Parameter	Observed Power[a]
Corrected Model	3767.772[b]	11	342.525	1.854	.047	.086	20.398	.868
Intercept	532053.491	1	532053.491	2880.381	.000	.930	2880.381	1.000
INTERNET	61.070	1	61.070	.331	.566	.002	.331	.088
INCOME	426.772	2	213.386	1.155	.317	.011	2.310	.252
EDUCATIO	1807.737	1	1807.737	9.787	.002	.043	9.787	.876
INTERNET * INCOME	366.772	2	183.386	.993	.372	.009	1.986	.222
INTERNET * EDUCATIO	200.860	1	200.860	1.087	.298	.005	1.087	.180
INCOME * EDUCATIO	151.895	2	75.947	.411	.663	.004	.822	.116
INTERNET * INCOME * EDUCATIO	752.667	2	376.333	2.037	.133	.019	4.075	.417
Error	39898.737	216	184.716					
Total	575720.000	228						
Corrected Total	43666.509	227						

[a] Computed using alpha = .05.
[b] R Squared = .086 (Adjusted R Squared = .040).

ESTIMATED MARGINAL MEANS

1. Grand Mean

Dependent Variable: NCE

		95% Confidence Interval	
Mean	Std. Error	Lower Bound	Upper Bound
48.307	.900	46.533	50.081

2. INTERNET

Dependent Variable: NCE

			95% Confidence Interval	
INTERNET	Mean	Std. Error	Lower Bound	Upper Bound
0	47.789	1.273	45.281	50.298
1	48.825	1.273	46.316	51.333

3. INCOME

Dependent Variable: NCE

			95% Confidence Interval	
INCOME	Mean	Std. Error	Lower Bound	Upper Bound
1	46.789	1.559	43.717	49.862
2	48.026	1.559	44.954	51.099
3	50.105	1.559	47.032	53.178

4. Education

Dependent Variable: NCE

Education	Mean	Std. Error	95% Confidence Interval	
			Lower Bound	Upper Bound
1	45.491	1.273	42.982	48.000
2	51.123	1.273	48.614	53.632

5. INTERNET * INCOME

Dependent Variable: NCE

INTERNET	INCOME	Mean	Std. Error	95% Confidence Interval	
				Lower Bound	Upper Bound
0	1	47.632	2.205	43.286	51.977
	2	47.842	2.205	43.497	52.188
	3	47.895	2.205	43.549	52.240
1	1	45.947	2.205	41.602	50.293
	2	48.211	2.205	43.865	52.556
	3	52.316	2.205	47.970	56.661

6. INTERNET * Education

Dependent Variable: NCE

INTERNET	Education	Mean	Std. Error	95% Confidence Interval	
				Lower Bound	Upper Bound
0	1	44.035	1.800	40.487	47.583
	2	51.544	1.800	47.996	55.092
1	1	46.947	1.800	43.399	50.496
	2	50.702	1.800	47.154	54.250

7. INCOME * Education

Dependent Variable: NCE

INCOME	Education	Mean	Std. Error	95% Confidence Interval	
				Lower Bound	Upper Bound
1	1	43.211	2.205	38.865	47.556
	2	50.368	2.205	46.023	54.714
2	1	46.342	2.205	41.997	50.688
	2	49.711	2.205	45.365	54.056
3	1	46.921	2.205	42.575	51.267
	2	53.289	2.205	48.944	57.635

8. INTERNET * INCOME * Education

Dependent Variable: NCE

INTERNET	INCOME	Education	Mean	Std. Error	95% Confidence Interval	
					Lower Bound	Upper Bound
0	1	1	40.842	3.118	34.697	46.988
		2	54.421	3.118	48.275	60.567
	2	1	45.316	3.118	39.170	51.461
		2	50.368	3.118	44.223	56.514
	3	1	45.947	3.118	39.802	52.093
		2	49.842	3.118	43.697	55.988
1	1	1	45.579	3.118	39.433	51.725
		2	46.316	3.118	40.170	52.461
	2	1	47.368	3.118	41.223	53.514
		2	49.053	3.118	42.907	55.198
	3	1	47.895	3.118	41.749	54.040
		2	56.737	3.118	50.591	62.882

Post Hoc Tests—INCOME

Multiple Comparisons

Dependent Variable:NCE

	(I) INCOME	(J) INCOME	Mean Difference (I-J)	Std. Error	Sig.	95% Confidence Interval	
						Lower Bound	Upper Bound
Scheffe	1	2	−1.24	2.205	.854	−6.67	4.20
		3	−3.32	2.205	.325	−8.75	2.12
	2	1	1.24	2.205	.854	−4.20	6.67
		3	−2.08	2.205	.642	−7.51	3.36
	3	1	3.32	2.205	.325	−2.12	8.75
		2	2.08	2.205	.642	−3.36	7.51
LSD	1	2	−1.24	2.205	.575	−5.58	3.11
		3	−3.32	2.205	.134	−7.66	1.03
	2	1	1.24	2.205	.575	−3.11	5.58
		3	−2.08	2.205	.347	−6.42	2.27
	3	1	3.32	2.205	.134	−1.03	7.66
		2	2.08	2.205	.347	−2.27	6.42
Dunnett T3	1	2	−1.24	2.138	.916	−6.40	3.93
		3	−3.32	2.377	.417	−9.05	2.42
	2	1	1.24	2.138	.916	−3.93	6.40
		3	−2.08	2.224	.726	−7.45	3.29
	3	1	3.32	2.377	.417	−2.42	9.05
		2	2.08	2.224	.726	−3.29	7.45

Based on observed means.

HOMOGENEOUS SUBSETS

NCE

	INCOME	N	Subset 1
Student-Newman-Keuls[a,b]	1	76	46.79
	2	76	48.03
	3	76	50.11
	Sig.		.291
Scheffe[a,b]	1	76	46.79
	2	76	48.03
	3	76	50.11
	Sig.		.325

Means for groups in homogeneous subsets are displayed.
Based on Type III Sum of Squares
The error term is Mean Square (Error) = 184.716.
[a] Uses Harmonic Mean Sample Size = 76.000.
[b] Alpha = .05.

APPENDIX V

ONE-WAY ANOVA—BALANCED DATA

ONE-WAY ANOVA ON FACTOR A (INTERNET) CALCULATED FROM BALANCED DATA

Descriptives

NCE

	N	Mean	Std. Deviation	Std. Error	95% Confidence Interval for Mean Lower Bound	95% Confidence Interval for Mean Upper Bound	Minimum	Maximum
0	114	47.79	13.367	1.252	45.31	50.27	18	78
1	114	48.82	14.395	1.348	46.15	51.50	14	84
Total	228	48.31	13.870	.919	46.50	50.12	14	84

Test of Homogeneity of Variances

NCE

Levene Statistic	df1	df2	Sig.
1.684	1	226	.196

ANOVA

NCE

	Sum of Squares	df	Mean Square	F	Sig.
Between Groups	61.070	1	61.070	.317	.574
Within Groups	43605.439	226	192.944		
Total	43666.509	227			

ONE-WAY ANOVA ON FACTOR B (INCOME) CALCULATED FROM BALANCED DATA

Descriptives

NCE

	N	Mean	Std. Deviation	Std. Error	95% Confidence Interval for Mean		Minimum	Maximum
					Lower Bound	Upper Bound		
1	76	46.79	14.161	1.624	43.55	50.03	18	78
2	76	48.03	12.124	1.391	45.26	50.80	21	75
3	76	50.11	15.133	1.736	46.65	53.56	14	84
Total	228	48.31	13.870	.919	46.50	50.12	14	84

Test of Homogeneity of Variances

NCE

Levene Statistic	df1	df2	Sig.
2.097	2	225	.125

ANOVA

NCE

	Sum of Squares	df	Mean Square	F	Sig.
Between Groups	426.772	2	213.386	1.110	.331
Within Groups	43239.737	225	192.177		
Total	43666.509	227			

POST HOC TESTS

Multiple Comparisons

Dependent Variable: NCE

	(I) INCOME	(J) INCOME	Mean Difference (I–J)	Std. Error	Sig.	95% Confidence Interval	
						Lower Bound	Upper Bound
Scheffe	1	2	−1.24	2.249	.860	−6.78	4.30
		3	−3.32	2.249	.339	−8.86	2.23
	2	1	1.24	2.249	.860	−4.30	6.78
		3	−2.08	2.249	.653	−7.62	3.46
	3	1	3.32	2.249	.339	−2.23	8.86
		2	2.08	2.249	.653	−3.46	7.62
LSD	1	2	−1.24	2.249	.583	−5.67	3.19
		3	−3.32	2.249	.142	−7.75	1.12
	2	1	1.24	2.249	.583	−3.19	5.67
		3	−2.08	2.249	.356	−6.51	2.35
	3	1	3.32	2.249	.142	−1.12	7.75
		2	2.08	2.249	.356	−2.35	6.51
Dunnett T3	1	2	−1.24	2.138	.916	−6.40	3.93
		3	−3.32	2.377	.417	−9.05	2.42
	2	1	1.24	2.138	.916	−3.93	6.40
		3	−2.08	2.224	.726	−7.45	3.29
	3	1	3.32	2.377	.417	−2.42	9.05
		2	2.08	2.224	.726	−3.29	7.45

Homogeneous Subsets

NCE

	INCOME	N	Subset for alpha =.05
			1
Student-Newman-Keuls[a]	1	76	46.79
	2	76	48.03
	3	76	50.11
	Sig.		.305
Scheffe[a]	1	76	46.79
	2	76	48.03
	3	76	50.11
	Sig.		.339

Means for groups in homogeneous subsets are displayed.
[a] Uses Harmonic Mean Sample Size = 76.000.

One-Way ANOVA on Factor B (Education) Calculated from Balanced Data

Descriptives

NCE

	N	Mean	Std. Deviation	Std. Error	95% Confidence Interval for Mean		Minimum	Maximum
					Lower Bound	Upper Bound		
1	114	45.49	13.147	1.231	43.05	47.93	18	71
2	114	51.12	14.056	1.316	48.51	53.73	14	84
Total	228	48.31	13.870	.919	46.50	50.12	14	84

Test of Homogeneity of Variances

NCE

Levene Statistic	df1	df2	Sig.
.005	1	226	.942

ANOVA

NCE

	Sum of Squares	df	Mean Square	F	Sig.
Between Groups	1807.737	1	1807.737	9.760	.002
Within Groups	41858.772	226	185.216		
Total	43666.509	227			

REFERENCES

Attewell, P., & Battle, J. (1999). Home Computers and School Performance. *The Information Society, 15*(1), 1–10. <http://www.ingentaconnect.com/content/tandf/utis/1999/00000015/00000001/art00002;jsessionid=3ojfjvmaa8doo.victoria> Retrieved October 13, 2004.

Becker, H. J. (2000). Who's Wired and Who's Not: Children's Access to and Use of Computer: Technology Children and Computer Technology. *The Future of Children, 10*(2), 44–75.

Bier, M. C. (1997). *Assessing the Effect of Unrestricted Home Internet Access on the Underserved Community: A Case Study of Four East Central Florida Families.* Doctoral dissertation, Florida Institute of Technology, 1997. Retrieved October 12, 2004, from Dissertation Abstracts Online.

Bruning, J. L., & Kintz, B. L. (1997). *Computational Handbook of Statistics.* Reading, MA: Addison-Wesley.

CTB / McGraw-Hill. (2004). *A Guide for Effective Assessment.* <http://www.ctb.com/articles/article_information.jsp?CONTENT%3C%3Ecnt_id=10134198673254779&FOLDER%3C%3Efolder_id=1408474395222381&bmUID=1106714628755> Retrieved January 25, 2005.

Davis, S. (2003). *An investigation of parental perceptions of and attitudes toward computer use in two predominantly Hispanic communities in the southwestern border region.* (Doctoral dissertation, New Mexico State University, 2003). Retrieved October 12, 2004, from Dissertation Abstracts Online.

Dickard, N. (Ed.). (2003). *The sustainability challenge: Taking ed-tech to the next level.* The Benton Foundation Communications Policy Program & EDC Center for Children and Technology. <http://www.benton.org/publibrary/sustainability/sus_challenge.pdf> Retrieved January 3, 2005.

Fairlie, R. (2003). *The Effects of Home computers on School Enrollment. JCPR Working Paper.* (Report No JCPR-WP-337). University of Chicago. Joint Center for Poverty Research.

Garson, G. D. (2005). *ANOVA.* <http://www2.chass.ncsu.edu/garson/pa765/anova.htm#levene> Retrieved May 22, 2005.

Gottfredson, L. (2004). *Interpreting Standardized Test Scores.* <http://www.udel.edu/educ/gottfredson/451/unit10-chap19.htm> Retrieved January 25, 2005.

Gregg. (2004). *Dr. Gregg's Testing & Measurement Corner, Tucson Unified School District.* <http://tusdstats.tusd.k12.az.us/planning/resources/dr_gregg/dr.html#nce> Retrieved January 25, 2005.

Hays, W. (1988). *Statistics* (4th ed.). New York: Holt, Rinehart and Winston, Inc.

Hernandez, M. (2003). *Database Design for Mere Mortals* (2nd ed.). Boston, MA: Pearson Education, Inc.

Horsley, R. (2004). *Factorial Arrangements.* <http://www.ndsu.nodak.edu/ndsu/ horsley/fact.pdf> Retrieved February 8, 2005.

Huang, J., & Russell, S. (2006). The digital divide and academic achievement. *The Electronic Library, 2*(24), 160–173. <http://www.emeraldinsight.com/ Insight/viewContentItem.do?contentType=Article&contentId=1552979> Retrieved September 12, 2006.

Indiana Department of Education. (2005). *Definition of Terms—NCE.* <http://www. doe.state.in.us/asap/definitions.html> Retrieved January 25, 2005.

Jackson, L. A., von Eye, A., Biocca, F. A., Barbatsis, G., & Zhao, Y. (2006). Does home Internet use influence the academic performance of low-income children? *Developmental Psychology, 3*(42). <http://www.apa.org/releases/dev423-jackson. pdf> Retrieved September 12, 2006.

Kafai, Y. B., Fishman, B. J., Bruckman, A. S., & Rockman, S. (2002). Models of Educational Computing @ Home: New Frontiers for Research on Technology in Learning. *Educational Technology Review, 10*(2), 52–68. <http://www.aace.org/ pubs/etr/issue3/Kafai.pdf> Retrieved February 19, 2005.

Lenhart, A., Simon, M., & Graziano, M. (2001). *The Internet & Education: Findings of the Pew Internet & American Life Project.* <http://www.pewinternet.org/reports/ toc.asp?Report=39> Retrieved January 12, 2005.

Levin, D., & Arafeh, S. (2002). *The Digital Disconnect: The Widening Gap between Internet-Savvy Students and Their Schools.* The Pew Internet & American Life Project. <http://www.pewinternet.org/pdfs/PIP_Schools_Internet_Report.pdf> Retrieved January 12, 2005.

McGraw-Hill. (2004). *CTB / McGraw-Hill—TerraNova, The Second Edition.* <http://www. ctb.com/netcaster/state_home.jsp?NC_ DIRECTORY%3C%3Edirectory_id=131& FOLDER%3C%3Efolder_id=1408474395214059&bmUID=1092808835513> Retrieved August 17, 2004.

McMillan-Culp, K., Honey, M., & Mandinach E. (2003). *A Retrospective on Twenty Years of Education Technology Policy.* U.S. Department of Education, Office of Educational Technology. <http://www.ed.gov/rschstat/eval/tech/20years.pdf> Retrieved October 13, 2004.

National Center for Educational Statistics. (2003). *Computer and Internet used by Children and Adolescents in 2001 Statistical Analysis Report.* The U.S. Department of Education, Institute of Educational Sciences and NCES 2004–014. <http://nces.ed.gov/pubs2004/2004014.pdf> Retrieved October 12, 2004.

———. (2004). *Digest of Statistical Tables and Figures–2003.* <http://nces.ed.gov/programs/digest/d03_tf.asp> Retrieved February 11, 2005.

New Mexico Public Education Department. (2004). *Focusing on Becoming Stronger: The State of Public Education in New Mexico—2003.* <http://www.ped.state.nm.us/resources/downloads/2003.annual.report.pdf> Retrieved January 25, 2005.

Nonnamaker, J. (2000). *Pre-college Internet use and freshman year academic achievement in a private college: The effect of sociodemographic characteristics, family socioeconomic status, academic ability and high school experiences.* (Doctoral dissertation, Fordham University, 2000). Retrieved October 12, 2004, from: Dissertation Abstracts Online.

Pennsylvania Department of Education. (2004). *Evaluation of Student & Parent Access through Recycled Computers.* <http://www.pde.state.pa.us/ed_tech/cwp/view.asp?A=169&Q=100397> Retrieved January 6, 2005.

Rathbun, A., West, J., & Hausken, E. (2003). Young Children's Access to Computers in the Home and at School in 1999 and 2000. *Education Statistics Quarterly, 5*(1), 25–30. National Center for Education Statistics, Institute of Education Sciences, U.S. Department of Education. <http://nces.ed.gov/pubsearch/pubsinfo.asp?pubid=2003036> Retrieved October 12, 2004.

San Miguel / New Mexico Highlands University GEARUP Partnership. (2004). *NMHU/San Miguel GEAR-UP Student Application, 2003–2004 School Year.* <http://gearup.nmhu.edu/par_stud/Student_Application_2003_2004.pdf> Retrieved February 05, 2005.

Schield, M. (1999). Statistical literacy: Thinking critically about statistics. *Of Significance* published *by The Association of Public Data Users, 1*(1), 1–7. <http://web.augsburg.edu/~schield/MiloPapers/984StatisticalLiteracy6.pdf> Retrieved October 12, 2004.

Toriskie, J. (1999). *The Effects of Internet Usage on Student Achievement and Student Attitudes (Fourth-Grade, Social Studies).* (Doctoral dissertation, Loyola University of Chicago, 1999). Retrieved October 12, 2004, from Dissertation Abstracts Online.

U.S. Department of Commerce. (2002). *A Nation Online: How Americans are Expanding their Use of the Internet.* Pew Internet Project Also, Economics and Statistics Administration, National Telecommunications and Information Administration. <http://www.ntia.doc.gov/ntiahome/dn/nationonline_020502.htm> Retrieved January 12, 2005.

U.S. Department of Education. (2001). *Archived Information: Gaining Early Aware-ness and Readiness for Undergraduate Programs (GEARUP)*. <http://www.ed.gov/pubs/AnnualPlan2002/rV185-GEARUP-0412.pdf> Retrieved January 12, 2005.

————. (2003). *Education Technology: Preparing Students and Parents for the Dig-ital Age.* <http://registerevent.ed.gov/downlink/event-flyer.asp?intEventID=168, 10,13,04> Retrieved October 12, 2004.

————. (2004). *Partnership Grants.* <http://www.ed.gov/programs/gearup/partner-ships-GA-NM.pdf> Retrieved January 26, 2005.

————. (2005a). *Toward A New Golden Age in American Education: How the Internet, the Law and Today's Students are Revolutionizing Expectations.* Office of Educational Technology. <http://www.nationaledtechplan.org/theplan/NETP_Final.pdf> Retrieved January 7, 2005.

————. (2005b). Gaining Early Awareness and Readiness for Undergraduate Programs (GEARUP), Washington, D.C. <http://www.ed.gov/programs/gearup> Retrieved January 25, 2005.

Warschauer, M., & Knobel, M. (2004). Technology and Equity in Schooling: Deconstructing the Digital Divide. *Educational Policy, 18*, 562–588.

Wearden, S., & Dowdy, S. 1991. *Statistics for Research* (2nd ed.). New York: John Wiley & Sons.

Webopedia. (2004). *Definition of GUID.* <http://www.webopedia.com/TERM/G/GUID.html> Retrieved October 12, 2004.

————. (2004). *Definition of the Internet.* <http://www.webopedia.com/TERM/I/Internet.html> Retrieved October 12, 2004.

Wielkiewicz, R. (2005). *Using SPSS for Windows.* <http://employees.csbsju.edu/rwielk/psy347/spssinst.htm> Retrieved May 22, 2005.

Winer, B. J. (1971). *Statistical Principles in Experimental Design* (2nd ed.). New York: McGraw Hill.

Name Index

Subject Index

Printed in the United States
81548LV00002BA/3